J10649854

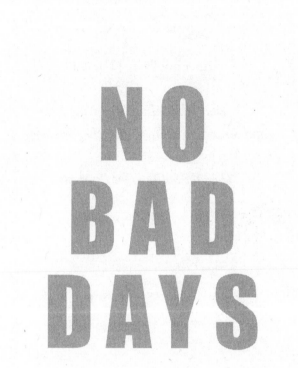

Other books by JT Jester

*Untether: Inspiration for Living Free
and Strong No Matter What the Challenge*

How the Sailfish Got Its Name

NO BAD DAYS

How to Find Joy in Any Circumstance

JT JESTER

Forefront
BOOKS

No Bad Days: How to Find Joy in Any Circumstance
© 2022 JT Mestdagh
All rights reserved.

No part of this book shall be reproduced or transmitted in any form or by any means, electronic, mechanical, magnetic, and photographic, including photocopying, recording or by any information storage and retrieval system, without prior written permission of the publisher.

No patent liability is assumed with respect to the use of the information contained herein. Although every precaution has been taken in the preparation of this book, the publisher and author assume no responsibility for errors or omissions. Neither is any liability assumed for damages resulting from the use of the information contained herein.

All Scripture quotations, unless otherwise indicated, are taken from the Holy Bible, New International Version®, NIV®. Copyright © 1973, 1978, 1984, 2011 by Biblica, Inc.® Used by permission of Zondervan. All rights reserved worldwide. www.zondervan.com. The "NIV" and "New International Version" are trademarks registered in the United States Patent and Trademark Office by Biblica, Inc.®

Scripture quotations marked NLT are taken from the Holy Bible, New Living Translation, copyright © 1996, 2004, 2015 by Tyndale House Foundation. Used by permission of Tyndale House Publishers, Carol Stream, Illinois 60188. All rights reserved.

Published by Forefront Books.

Cover Design by Bruce Gore, Gore Studio Inc.
Interior Design by Mary Susan Oleson, Blu Design Concepts

ISBN: 978-1-63763-057-0 print
ISBN: 978-1-63763-058-7 e-book

TO MY PARENTS, who taught me to get up when I fell down, to believe in myself when others didn't, to push myself to my limits, to conquer my goals, and, most importantly, to be nice to others.

Contents

Introduction

IMAGINE YOU'VE TRAVELED to a foreign country, and you're completely lost. You have no idea how to communicate in the native language. You don't know which restroom is for men and which is for women. You can't read a street sign. You can't read the names on storefronts. You can't read a newspaper and don't understand what people are saying on television.

Imagine that you're visiting China and can't read a menu to tell the waiter that you'd like to order tofu or Peking duck for dinner. Or imagine that during a business trip to Mexico, you're suddenly in distress but can't read the sign outside the *policía* station. Every single word you see and hear seems so foreign, and you have absolutely no idea what any of them means.

Now imagine that is how you spend every day of your life.

For many of the estimated 43.5 million Americans who have some form of dyslexia, seemingly simple tasks such as reading, writing, and speaking might seem impossible.[1] They struggle to learn letters and sounds. They can't memorize numbers and facts. They process words and sentences too slowly to comprehend what they just read. Reading novels, magazine articles, and long books might feel like they're trying to ascend Mount Kilimanjaro, and subjects like math, chemistry, and foreign languages present entirely different challenges.

Trust me, I know exactly how they feel.

On October 8, 2018, after a grueling four-day climb, I reached the 19,341-foot-tall peak of Mount Kilimanjaro, the tallest mountain in Africa and the highest single freestanding mountain in the world. Roughly 35,000 people attempt to climb Mount Kilimanjaro every year, and about one-third of them turn back because of altitude sickness, injury, or poor weather.[2] Each year, rescuers evacuate approximately one thousand climbers from Mount Kilimanjaro, and an average of ten deaths are reported due to high-altitude illness, falling, or other trauma.[3]

Reaching Mount Kilimanjaro's majestic, snow-covered summit was an accomplishment that changed my life forever. It gave twenty-three-year-old me the confidence and self-assurance I could do anything I put my mind to. It taught me that no matter what challenge God decided to throw my way, I could accomplish it with slow, steady steps, patience, and resilience. That day on that mountaintop, I learned that when we overcome an obstacle, we build amazing qualities like perseverance, stamina, grit, and accountability.

No matter how difficult life might feel sometimes, it's always possible to reach the summit.

As demanding as Mount Kilimanjaro was, for me it was nothing compared to learning to read. I'm among those estimated 43.5 million Americans who have dyslexia. I also have short-term memory loss, which makes my condition worse. You can't reverse dyslexia.

No matter how difficult life might feel sometimes, it's always possible to reach the summit.

It's a lifelong condition that can be treated with tutoring, therapy, and systematic and structured teaching methods. With early identification and the proper help, most people with dyslexia eventually learn to read and write. It's a long, slow struggle—and it was especially hard for me.

Despite what you might have read or what others have told you in the past, people with dyslexia don't see reversed letters and numbers. Because we process information using parts of our brain that are different from those most people use, words and sounds appear jumbled. Our brains have difficulty recognizing phonemes like the *b* sound in bat or the *s* sound in Sam. That makes it difficult to blend those sounds into words. Car might look like *arc* to me. Dog might look like *God*. Left might look like *felt*. You get the idea. Making matters worse, after I've worked extra hard to sound out letters to read a word, I might forget what I just learned only a short time later.

In addition to my learning differences, I faced many physical problems as a child. I weighed five pounds, two ounces when I was born in Detroit on September 13, 1995. When I came out of my mother's womb, my skin and lips were blue. My mother heard someone say, "Cut the cord!" Nurses took me to the neonatal intensive care unit. My parents, Kristine and Jim Mestdagh, had to wait a week to hold me for the first time.

The day after I was born, Dr. Fredrick E. Rector used a tiny pair of surgical scissors to save my life for the first of many times. By the time I was three years old, I had spent 250 days in the hospital. During my first sixteen years on earth, I endured sixteen major surgeries, two of which were to correct a tethered spinal cord that might have caused permanent paralysis. Surgeons deconstructed and reconstructed my abdomen; eighteen inches of my colon were removed. Surgeons have cut me from the top of my chest to below my waistline. And, yes, doctors eventually gave me a functioning anus, if you were wondering.

As painful as some of those surgeries and recoveries were for me, nothing was as emotionally draining and frustrating as trying to learn to read and write. On top of that, because of my short-term memory loss, learning was even more difficult for me. So much so that when I was in the fifth grade, my parents were called to a meeting in which a psychologist told them I'd be illiterate for the rest of my life. A few months later, an administrator told me I could no longer go to school there.

Remember what I said about overcoming any obstacle? Yes, a door was slammed in my face. But my parents refused to keep it closed. Over the next seven years, I would learn that God wants to open doors for us. We only have to let go and allow Him to have His way. We must not only pray for God to open doors for us, we must also pray for Him to close doors in our lives that need to be shut. In the following pages, you'll read about the many doors that He has opened for others and me.

As Revelation 3:8 tells us, "I know your deeds. See, I have placed before you an open door that no one can shut. I know that you have little strength, yet you have kept my word and have not denied my name."

My parents' faith allowed me to endure my early struggles. They taught me that circumstances in life can make you bitter or better, and I've always been a glass-half-full kind of guy. Over time, I became

> *There are no bad days, only hard days.*

stronger in my faith in God, which made me more confident and self-assured. I knew God had a plan for my life. As I've told my dad so many times, there are no bad days, only hard days.

Difficult and trying times mold us into who we are, and it's up to each of us to decide whether those lessons are good or bad. Throughout the following pages, I'm going to share some of the core values I've learned along the way, including:

Find Your Tribe: I learned at an early age that it's critical to surround yourself with people who push you, give you courage, and have your back. God didn't design humans to be lone wolves. That's why there were two people in the Garden of Eden. It's important to understand that we need other people in our lives to engage us, encourage us, and love us.

Every single day, you should be finding your tribe. You can't do life alone.

Learn and Don't Stop: It's amazing what I've been forced to learn over the first quarter-century of my life. I've learned about parts of my body I didn't even know existed. I've learned about how my brain operates and processes information. I'm learning new skills and techniques each day, and I've learned that

I must continually seek new ways to improve myself and to live my life to the fullest. Most importantly, I'm always learning more and more about my relationship with God.

Listen to Others: How many times in our lives have we thought to ourselves: *If I had only listened . . . ?* If only we had listened to a friend who needed help, we might have helped protect that friend from harm. If only we had written down the entire grocery list, we wouldn't have had to go back to the store again. If only we had listened to directions, we would have found our destination the first time instead of driving in circles for hours.

Speak in such a way that others will want to listen to you, and listen in such a way that others will want to talk to you. Listening is an attitude, so if you have a bad attitude, chances are, you won't listen.

Take Off Your Mask: Given what we have endured over the many long months of the coronavirus pandemic, you might think I'm talking about the blue surgical masks or fancier cloth face coverings we have been forced to wear everywhere.

No, I'm talking about another kind of mask—the one that is preventing you from being the authentic and original person God wants you to be. Being authentic and original isn't easy. Trust me, I know how uncomfortable and scary it is to stick to your faith, morals, and values in the face of peer pressure and societal changes. Ask yourself what you truly believe, what your parents might have taught you to believe, and what God wants you to believe. Look in the mirror and evaluate whether you are truly happy with the person you have become. When you're not authentic, the only person you are fooling is yourself.

Stretch Yourself: Later on, you will read about the most challenging physical ailment I had to deal with—twice—while growing up. It is called a tethered spine. When the spinal cord is pulled down and becomes fixed to the spinal canal, it creates a very serious condition.

In life, we have to learn to stretch ourselves, even if that means we open ourselves up to the possibility of failure. We must learn to be comfortable with being uncomfortable. Once we realize it's okay to color outside the lines, we will stretch ourselves to try new things, meet new people, acquire new tastes, and truly explore the world and all of God's creations.

Pull Off the Label: When I was a kid, one of the things I despised most was when others—some of whom didn't even know me—placed a label on me. They threw around labels that could be hurtful, especially for a young man who was struggling with his health and learning differences. You know the words I'm talking about: dumb, different, slow, stupid . . . or worse.

Our society loves to label people, whether it's describing physical appearances, political leanings, personalities, sexual orientation, or just about anything else. We must remember that people are human beings and not things. It's okay to label items in a grocery store or to put warning labels on things that might harm us, but labels should never be used to describe people.

Tell Your Story: The next time you find yourself on a busy street or in a crowded room (and hopefully, that's sometime soon), look at the people surrounding you. Each one of them has a story, and there's a reason they are the way they are. Every one of us has gone through something that impacted us, whether it was good or bad. Each of our stories is unique, genuine, and real, and every one of them needs to be told.

I had a story to tell, and it's why I'm telling it now. If my parents hadn't spoken up for me when I was a child, I would have never learned to read or write. If I hadn't shared my story with teachers and professors when I was older, I would have never completed high school and college.

The common thread that runs through each of these core values I discussed is kindness. I fear it's become a forgotten trait among us humans. If I had the power, I'd buy and send an ounce of kindness to every person on earth. We could use a lot more kindness around the world.

> *Each of our stories is unique, genuine, and real, and every one of them needs to be told.*

Scientific studies have shown that being kind make us feel better about ourselves and more satisfied with our own lives.[4] It's not difficult to be kind. Carry someone's groceries. Open a door for a stranger. Compliment a colleague's hard work. Encourage a friend who might be struggling. Pay for a stranger's coffee or lunch. Tutor a young person who needs help. Send a long-lost friend a card, email, or flowers. Volunteer at a soup kitchen or homeless shelter. Thank a police officer or emergency responder.

See? Being kind isn't too hard. It only takes a little initiative and effort. So be kind out there. We need it now more than ever.

I hope my story inspires you to tell your own—I'd love to hear it. In the meantime, I hope you enjoy reading mine.

CHAPTER ONE

Tell Your Story

SHORTLY AFTER I was born, one of the nurses at St. John Hospital and Medical Center in Detroit handed my parents a single sheet of paper. There were eleven paragraphs and fewer than four hundred words in the essay, written in typewriter font, like the kind produced by an old Smith Corona. The words were faded, as if the essay had been photocopied millions of times for parents around the world who had given birth to a child with physical differences.

My parents, Jim and Kristine Mestdagh, were married four years before I was born. My mother's pregnancy had gone well. I was born three weeks early, after Mom's water broke at 3:20 AM on September 13, 1995. When that happened, Mom tried to go back to sleep, while Dad, who has a more-than-mild but undiagnosed case of obsessive-compulsive disorder, started cleaning their house and doing laundry.

They arrived at the hospital around seven o'clock that morning, and after nearly half a day of labor (she still hasn't forgiven me), the doctors finally gave Mom an epidural around 5:30. There were twelve specialists in the birthing room while my parents anxiously waited for me to come out. There were no indications on ultrasounds and other tests that there was anything wrong with me during Mom's pregnancy. But during labor, her OB-GYN sensed something was wrong so he started calling various specialists into the room. Finally, I was born at 8:07 PM, weighing five pounds, two ounces.

* * *

After a very long day, which ended with me in the NICU, my parents were worried and exhausted. Unfortunately, Mom was in quite a bit of pain because a doctor had nicked her spinal column when he was administering the epidural. After consulting with the doctors, Dad decided to go home to get some sleep and let Mom rest. He still wasn't aware of the full extent of my health issues, but he was becoming more and more concerned.

Before Dad went to bed that night, he silently prayed, asking God for reassurance that everything would be okay. He pulled his Bible from the nightstand and opened it. The pages fell to the tenth chapter of the Gospel of Mark:

> People were bringing little children to Jesus for him to place his hands on them, but the disciples rebuked them. When Jesus saw this, he was indignant. He said to them, "Let the

little children come to me, and do not hinder them, for the kingdom of God belongs to such as these. Truly I tell you, anyone who will not receive the kingdom of God like a little child will never enter it." And he took the children in his arms, placed his hands on them and blessed them. (10:13–16)

Those were the exact words my father needed to read at that very moment, and all these years later, Dad is still convinced that God's hands opened his Bible to that particular passage. Dad knew God was speaking to him, letting him know that He would take me in His arms, place His hands on me, and bless me. Dad felt comforted and reassured. After reading the passage, Dad knew in his heart that God loved his children, and that no matter what, God loved me.

God loved his children, and no matter what, God loved me.

The next morning, my parents learned the frightening specifics of my condition. My trachea and esophagus were conjoined; a blocked trachea meant I couldn't get oxygen to my lungs and would suffocate. Beyond that, my upper esophagus wasn't connected to my lower esophagus and my stomach, meaning I couldn't get food and fluids from my mouth to my stomach. Doctors inserted a temporary feeding tube through my nose to my stomach to feed me. I also had an imperforate anus, which meant I couldn't use the restroom like everyone else. About one in every five thousand infants is born with a misplaced or blocked rectal opening, and I would need a colostomy to help me pass solids for the time being.[5]

Doctors needed to do emergency surgery to fix my trachea and esophagus and to disconnect my colon from my rectum and reroute my colon to two stomas. It was a very risky procedure for an infant who wasn't yet a day old.

Feeling worried and sad, Dad went to the neonatal intensive care unit to get another look at his sick son. While washing his hands and putting on scrubs, Dad overheard a doctor talking to two grieving parents. The doctors advised the young couple that the hospital could help them make funeral arrangements for their baby. Immediately, Dad stopped feeling sorry for himself. He was happy that I was alive, whatever condition I was in, and he knew that God would protect me and keep me safe.

On September 14, 1995, Dr. Fredrick E. Rector performed a nearly five-hour surgery to save my life. With his God-given talent and wisdom, Dr. Rector cleared my windpipe, reconnected my esophagus to my stomach, and inserted a colostomy to help me use the bathroom. Dr. Rector saved my life, but my parents and I still faced a very long road to recovery and health.

Eventually, doctors diagnosed me with having VATER Syndrome, which is a combination of several birth defects that often occur in conjunction with one another and impact vertebrae, anus, trachea, esophagus, and kidneys. Infants with at least three of these birth defects are diagnosed with VATER Syndrome.[6] I was lucky enough to have all five. My parents didn't change diapers during the first year of my life. They changed a colostomy bag.

Fifteen days after I was born, I was finally ready to go home. My parents were ready to leave the hospital too. Before we left, a nurse gave my parents a copy of the faded sheet of paper that I told you about earlier. It was an essay titled, "Welcome to Holland," and it would have a profound impact on them like it has on so many other parents around the world. Here is that short yet powerful essay:

> I am often asked to describe the experience of raising a child with a disability—to try to help people who have not shared that unique experience to understand it, to imagine how it would feel. It's like this:
>
> When you're going to have a baby, it's like planning a fabulous vacation trip—to

Italy. You buy a bunch of guide books and make your wonderful plans. The Colosseum. The Michelangelo *David*. The gondolas in Venice. You may learn some handy phrases in Italian. It's all very exciting.

After months of eager anticipation, the day finally arrives. You pack your bags and off you go. Several hours later, the plane lands. The stewardess comes in and says, "Welcome to Holland."

"Holland?!" you say. "What do you mean Holland? I signed up for Italy! I'm supposed to be in Italy. All my life I've dreamed of going to Italy."

But there's been a change in the flight plan. They've landed in Holland, and there you must stay.

The important thing is that they haven't taken you to a horrible, disgusting, filthy place, full of pestilence, famine, and disease. It's just a different place.

So you must go out and buy new guide books. And you must learn a whole new language. And you will meet a whole new group of people you would never have met.

It's just a different place. It's slower-paced than Italy, less flashy than Italy. But after you've been there for a while and you catch your breath, you look around, and you begin to notice that Holland has windmills . . . and Holland has tulips. Holland even has Rembrandts.

But everyone you know is busy coming and going from Italy, and they're all bragging about what a wonderful time they had there. And for the rest of your life, you will say, "Yes, that's where I was supposed to go. That's what I had planned."

And the pain of that will never, ever, ever, ever go away—because the loss of that dream is a very, very significant loss.

But if you spend your life mourning the fact that you didn't get to Italy, you may never be free to enjoy the very special, the very lovely things—about Holland.[7]

Emily Perl Kingsley, an award-winning writer for *Sesame Street* for forty-five years until her retirement in 2015, wrote "Welcome to Holland" in 1987. Thirteen years earlier, Emily and her husband, Charles, had given birth to their son Jason, who was born with Down syndrome. Down syndrome is a genetic condition that affects about one in every seven hundred babies in the United States every year, according to the National Down Syndrome Society. Babies born with Down syndrome have forty-seven chromosomes, instead of

> *God knits us together exactly how He wants us to be, and He doesn't make mistakes.*

the usual forty-six, with three copies (instead of the usual two) of chromosome 21. The probability of having a child with Down syndrome is higher among mothers over the age of thirty-four.[8]

While Emily Kingsley and her husband might have ended up in Holland, instead of Italy as they had planned, Jason's birth was no mistake. His parents might not have planned for a baby born with Down syndrome, just as my parents hadn't prepared for a son born with so many health problems. But I know in my heart and soul that God had planned for Jason and me all along, and He was not at all surprised by our births. God knits us together exactly how He wants us to be, and He doesn't make mistakes. In Psalm 139:13–16, we read:

> For you created my inmost being;
>   you knit me together in my mother's womb.
> I praise you because I am fearfully and
>   wonderfully made;
>   your works are wonderful,

I know that full well.
My frame was not hidden from you
  when I was made in the secret place,
  when I was woven together in the depths
of the earth.
You eyes saw my unformed body;
  all the days ordained for me were written
in your book
  before one of them came to be.

God chose my parents for me, and He chose me for them. We are God's gifts to our parents, and our parents are His gifts to us. I believe that God has a plan and purpose for people like Jason and me—and our parents.

Do you know what the most amazing thing about Jason's story is? Shortly after he was born, an obstetrician told his mother that he wouldn't walk, talk, or learn. In fact, the doctor said he should be institutionalized, which was what society did with a lot of children with Down syndrome and other developmental differences back then. The doctor even gave his mother pills to dry up her breast milk.[9]

"His recommendation was that I not feed him, hold him, or get attached to him—but to send him to an institution and tell our friends and family that he had died in childbirth," Emily told *People* in 1994.[10]

Fortunately, Emily and Charles wouldn't listen

to the doctor's advice, and neither would Jason's two older brothers, who told their mom, "Of course, you are going to bring him home. He's our brother."[11]

Emily became Jason's biggest supporter and was determined to provide him with a life of happiness, independence, and fulfillment. When he was a baby, according to *People*, she sewed a quilt made of fabrics of different textures to give him different touch sensations. She painted his nursery in bright colors and prepared forty boxes of Jell-O and mixed them in a large roasting pan. She sat Jason in the sweet concoction and let him smell and taste the rainbow of colors. Jason started reading when he was four and could count in twelve languages by age seven, according to Emily.[12] Jason's parents took him to Broadway musicals, and he memorized the lyrics to songs.[13]

Emily became an ardent advocate for people born with Down syndrome and other differences. She cast people with differences on *Sesame Street*, including Tarah Schaeffer, an actress who uses a wheelchair.[14] Jason appeared on *Sesame Street* for the first time when he was fifteen months old.[15] In 1977, Jason's story was the subject of an hour-long NBC special called *This Is My Son*, and in 1987, Emily wrote the script for *Kids Like These*, a made-for-TV movie about a middle-aged couple who had a son with Down syndrome.[16]

Instead of spending his life in a dark and dreary mental institution, as his mother's obstetrician had recommended, Jason grew up in a loving and supporting home. He graduated from high school, attended post-secondary school,[17] and became an actor. He appeared in popular TV series including *Sesame Street*, *The Fall Guy*, *All My Children*, and *Touched by an Angel*.[18] Jason and his friend Mitchell Levitz wrote a book called *Count Us In: Growing Up with Down Syndrome*. Emily typed their words into a manuscript—unedited—because she wanted to share with readers their unique thoughts and conversations. The most wonderful thing I've read about Jason is that he told *People* that Down syndrome should be called "Up" syndrome because it's more positive.[19]

In an interview in 2019, Emily said she wrote the "Welcome to Holland" essay after talking to a mother who had just had a baby with Down syndrome. She explained:

> I found myself telling her what it was like and out came this spontaneous analogy. . . . When I got home later I thought about it and realized that she had responded to our conversation and it had a positive impact on the new mom and it worked for her, made her feel a little better. I said to myself, "That's not bad. I ought to write that down."

I did and mentioned it again to another new family a couple of weeks later. Shortly after that I was writing my CBS Movie-of-the-Week *Kids Like These* and decided to use it as the concluding scene of the movie. After that it sort of "went viral," as they say, and the rest is history. It just "took off."[20]

By telling Jason's story and sharing his uplifting message through TV and "Welcome to Holland," Emily has inspired countless parents around the world, most of whom probably never expected to end up in Holland when their children were born. Jason's life and his parents' love for him are the perfect example of why it's so important to tell your story. Few things are as valuable or more beneficial than telling your story to others. You never know who might be inspired or helped by hearing your story. If we don't tell our stories, we can never celebrate the struggles and obstacles we've overcome in our lives.

My parents were among the people who were truly touched and inspired by Emily's words. In fact, my father keeps a copy of the essay in his office desk. From time to time, he pulls the letter out and reads it silently; her words still bring him comfort and motivation to support me and help others. My parents were especially drawn to the essay because my maternal grandfather, John Boll, is the son of Dutch immigrants who came to America as young newly-weds who couldn't speak a lick of English (you'll read more about him later). As Papi likes to say, "If you're not Dutch, you're not much!"

While my parents might have been forced to buy new guide books, learn an entirely new language, and meet a whole new group of people they never expected to know, they quickly learned that Holland wasn't a

If we don't tell our stories, we can never celebrate the struggles and obstacles we've overcome in our lives.

"disgusting, filthy place, full of pestilence, famine, and disease." Yes, I'll admit that it was different from what they were expecting, and at times it was quite messy thanks to the colostomy bag. But because of God's love and their devotion to each other and me, our lives together have been special. And while I endured much pain and many surgeries over the years, I'm now a mostly healthy, athletic young man who loves to snow ski, hike, climb mountains, bike, and go boating.

Much like Emily Perl Kingsley was for her son,

my parents are my biggest advocates. When I was a young boy, they were my voice—and they shared my story loudly. When others tried to close a door, they stuck out their feet to keep it open. And when they realized the medical and developmental problems I would soon be facing, they were determined to find people who could help me.

CHAPTER TWO

Pray for Someone

....

FAITH IS A very important part of my family's story. My parents grew up in Christian homes, and they pray and read the Bible regularly. We attended church as a family almost every Sunday when I was a kid, and still do today.

My mother, Kristine, loves reading daily devotionals from *Our Daily Bread*, a calendar-style booklet printed in more than fifty-five languages by Our Daily Bread Ministries in Grand Rapids, Michigan.[21] *Our Daily Bread* has been around for more than sixty years,[22] and it has brought countless people to Jesus Christ through its mission to make "the life-changing wisdom of the Bible understandable and accessible to all." The devotionals include scripture and a short story written by a different author each day.

I was born on Wednesday, September 13, 1995, and that morning my mother read a devotional titled, "Trust Him with Your Heart." The Bible passage is Proverbs 15:29, which says, "The LORD is far from the wicked, but he hears the prayer of the righteous."

The story was about sportswriter Watson "Waddy" Spoelstra and his wife, Jean. She had been suffering from congestive heart failure for three years. During a

> *"The LORD is far from the wicked, but he hears the prayer of the righteous."*
>
> PROVERBS 15:29

follow-up exam, her doctor was surprised that her heart was suddenly strong and her lungs were clear.

"Praise the Lord!" Waddy shouted out loud.

"That's it," the doctor told Waddy and Jean. "You two have positive attitudes. You believe in answered prayer. As I've said before, prayer is a big part of medical care."[23]

Waddy Spoelstra knew the power of prayer very well. The well-known sportswriter was a recovering alcoholic and born-again Christian.[24] In 1957, Spoelstra's eighteen-year-old daughter suffered a brain hemorrhage and fell into a coma. Waddy dropped to his knees and offered his life to God if He would heal her. Miraculously, Waddy's daughter recovered, and he followed through on his promise to God.[25]

Waddy was a beat writer for the *Detroit News* for nearly three decades and wrote about the sports stars of his day, including boxer Joe Louis and Olympic champion Jesse Owens.[26] I'm sure my paternal grandfather, Bill Mestdagh, who is a big sports fan, grew up reading Waddy's stories about the Detroit Lions, Tigers, and Red Wings and his beloved Michigan Wolverines.

Waddy covered a lot of different sports in his storied writing career, but baseball was his first love. He was president of the Baseball Writers' Association of America in 1968.[27] Waddy's lasting legacy in America's game occurred five years later when he asked Major League Baseball commissioner Bowie Kuhn if he could organize a chapel service for every team. Kuhn signed off on the idea, and with the help of baseball stars Hank Aaron and Tommy John, manager Sparky Anderson, and Tigers broadcaster Ernie Harwell, Waddy's vision became a reality.[28]

By the start of the 1975 season, every Major League team had a chapel service.[29] Waddy understood the importance of faith and the power of prayer, and still today hundreds of players in the major leagues, minor leagues, and winter leagues in Puerto Rico, Venezuela, Mexico, Japan, Nicaragua, and the Dominican Republic participate in chapel services every week.[30]

Waddy and Jean Spoelstra were married for fifty-nine years until her death in 1998.[31] He died at age eighty-nine the next year. Their son, Jon, was an executive in the National Basketball Association, and their grandson, Erik, is the head coach of the NBA's Miami Heat. Erik won two NBA world championships while coaching LeBron James and Dwayne Wade in 2012 and 2013.[32]

As Mom read the story that morning, she didn't realize that she would have to steadfastly believe in the power of prayer and trust God with all her heart in the coming days, weeks, months, and years.

As I said earlier, I was born with VATER Syndrome, which is a set of three to five birth defects that occur together. I had all five. Children who are also born with heart and limb defects are diagnosed with VACTERL syndrome. My heart and limbs were fine.

It is unclear how the specific birth defects associated with VATER Syndrome are connected. Scientists and doctors believe the condition is probably caused by genetics. It's extremely rare—about one in every ten to forty thousand children is diagnosed with VATER. Unfortunately, there are no pre-birth or genetic tests that diagnose or predict the condition.[33]

I was diagnosed with VATER on the first day of my life and spent my first five days on a ventilator. Since I was so sick, I was monitored in the neonatal intensive care unit twenty-four hours a day. My parents were blindsided, but because of their faith they say they didn't immediately question why their son had to be the sickly one. They knew God is in charge, that nothing happens without His direction, and that He has a plan for our lives. Wherever that plan took my parents and me, we had to trust that it would be perfect and good.

The morning of my first surgery, Mom pulled out *Our Daily Bread* and read another devotional. It was titled, "The Cure for Resentment." It was the story of Peter and John. When Jesus told the apostle Peter that he was going to die as a martyr, Peter asked why John wasn't facing the same fate. Peter didn't think it was fair that John didn't have to die for his faith too. Jesus explained that it wasn't Peter's concern what happened to John. Their fate was God's will, and Peter's responsibility as a Christian was to follow Christ.[34]

After my mother read that devotional, she and my father began to understand the power of prayer and why they had given birth to a sick child. It was for a specific reason—it was God's will. Life isn't always fair, but we can't be resentful that we might be facing more obstacles and hardships than others. Many parents bring healthy babies into the world, while others help their children overcome differences, disease, and sickness. Life is short. Spending time feeling angry or resentful about what did or didn't happen is only time wasted. Focus on what you have, not what you don't, and you'll realize how blessed you truly are.

My parents quickly learned that in our weakest moments, we might feel like no one else knows what we're going through. My parents had each other but sometimes felt isolated during what should have been

Focus on what you have, not what you don't, and you'll realize how blessed you truly are.

the happiest time of their lives. They couldn't show off their new baby boy to family and friends because I was in the NICU. Because I was born three weeks early, Dad attended a previously scheduled baby shower for Mom. He could only show her friends a Polaroid photograph of me. There was a feeding tube in my nose, heart monitors on my chest, and a panda sticker covering my navel.

Some of my parents' friends didn't call or visit because they didn't know how to act or what to say to someone who had just given birth to a sick child. My parents didn't have all the answers either. They were scared and confused, but they put my life in God's hands. (We have to remember that God knows our feelings and frustrations—and our fears.) God not only knows, but He cares. As it says in Psalm 56:8, "You keep track of all my sorrows. You have collected all my tears in your bottle. You have recorded each one in your book" (NLT).

My parents became stronger in their faith and belief in the power of prayer, and a lot of good people were praying for me in those first few days. Mom kept all of the cards and letters they received after I was born (this was a few years before email became popular), and the handwritten messages offered them encouragement, comfort, and love.

In one card, my Aunt Tee wrote that after a conversation with Mom, she read Philippians 4:13, which says, "I can do all this through him who gives me strength." Aunt Tee also said:

> You and Jim have been so faithful through this challenge; it has been an encouragement to us who believe, and as I mentioned and you did, too, to those who don't know the Lord. I know through this that you and Jim will grow closer to the Lord with the help of prayer and the Bible, but closer to one another too! The Lord will continue to bless you who are faithful, this we know because He tells us so![35]

In another letter, family friend Robert Fawcett wrote:

> I know your faith is strong, but sometimes our faith can be tested to the threshold, especially when our firstborn has either a life-threatening problem or a quality of life problem. "Why me? Why us? Why my baby?" A favorite observation of mine is that we all have our

Christ-centered (Christian) taught beliefs, but many people either do not have or lose faith in those same beliefs when the goin' gets tough. While the scare may be over with, the trick is to reflect on what we've been taught by Jesus and surround yourselves with Christian brothers and sisters in a time of need. Just remember this: aside from our Father, in a time of need, you have people like us as family friends, your parents (both sides), and above all, each other. Be thankful. Strengthen your faith. Pray.[36]

I would argue that I'm living proof of the power of prayer, and I've witnessed the power of prayer so many times since then. How many times have you been asked to join a Facebook group to pray for a sick child, someone seriously injured in a car accident, or a parent or grandparent fighting for their lives? CaringBridge.org, a website that has built "bridges of care and communication providing love and support on a health journey" since 1997, has published over 850,000 sites for someone in need of help and prayer. According to CaringBridge, a new website is created for someone experiencing a health crisis every twelve minutes.[37] You're telling me people don't believe in the power of prayer? We're all going to pass away one day, but hopefully it brings families hope and peace to know that others are praying for them when they are fighting these battles.

People turn to prayer and God during the worst of times, and that was never more evident than during the coronavirus pandemic. How many stories have you read online or watched on TV in which a COVID-19 survivor has credited his or her recovery to faith in God and prayers from others? Nic Brown, a thirty-eight-year-old Ohio man who nearly died from COVID-19 and was put on a ventilator and life support, walked out of the hospital and said, "I truly believe faith made the difference and the power of prayer and the people behind me just pouring over me the prayers that they were giving me."[38]

Clay Bentley, a Georgia man in his late fifties who became sick with COVID-19 after singing in a one-hundred-person church choir, was put in isolation and only had contact with nurses in PPE gear. On his sixth night in the hospital, his lungs filled with fluid, and he couldn't breathe.[39] Clay's family and friends prayed for his recovery. "And then all of a sudden I felt breath going into me," the man said. "It was the Lord on top of my chest. When he breathed into me I felt the power of God hit me."[40] Clay left the hospital two days later.

Ramon Zuniga, a fifty-year-old man from Torrance, California, spent twenty-eight days in the ICU and twenty of those days in a medically induced coma on a ventilator as he fought COVID-19. He lost sixty pounds while fighting the disease. On Easter Sunday 2020, Zuniga left the hospital and went home.

> *We're living, breathing proof of the power of prayer and prayers of intercession.*

His family saluted the brave doctors and nurses who cared for him and helped save his life, but they also thanked God and the people who were praying for him. "This is a complete and total miracle," his wife said. "One thing that helped us through this is we are very faithful to God and we had so many people, who we didn't even know, including us in their prayers."[41]

We're living, breathing proof of the power of prayer and prayers of intercession. Aren't those amazing stories of hope, recovery, and faith to tell and share?

Whom can you pray for? When we feel inadequate and helpless to assist others in overcoming their obstacles like disease, drug addiction, injury, financial distress, and other problems, we can't forget that we have the power of prayer. Praying helps us become more empathetic toward their struggles and puts us in their shoes. Most importantly, when we pray for others, we are doing what God wants us to do by demonstrating His love, mercy, and compassion. Pray for others with love and do it from the heart. If nothing else, it's the kind thing to do.

CHAPTER THREE

Serve Others

....

IN AUGUST 1996, about a month before my first birthday, Dr. Fredrick Rector reversed my colostomy using a "pull-through" surgery, a technique that was developed and perfected by world-renowned surgeon Dr. Alberto Peña.[42] Following the surgery at the Children's Hospital of Michigan, Dr. Rector remarked that he had "made the perfect asshole."

In my hospital bed the next night, I seized for two minutes. My lips turned blue, my mouth foamed, and my body turned stiff. Another four-minute seizure came in the middle of the night. My lungs filled with fluid and collapsed. Over the next few days, doctors stabilized me, and I was able to go home about a week later.

While I finally had a perfectly functioning anus, the rest of my plumbing still wasn't working properly. I didn't have the muscles needed to push food through my esophagus, stomach, intestines, and colon. Gravity was the only thing helping push the food along. I was jaundiced, lethargic, and not growing like other kids my age because my body wasn't absorbing nutrients or getting rid of waste.

My parents and doctors tried everything to make my plumbing work—chiropractors, reflexologists, massage therapists, herbal therapy, laxatives, enemas—but nothing made things better. My bowels were clogged. Mom was so concerned that she called Grace Fenton, a family friend, and told her to pray for me because my little body wasn't fighting back.

> *My parents and doctors tried everything to make my plumbing work.*

Finally, Dr. Rector, who later became our neighbor and a close family friend, contacted Dr. Peña, who was the chief of pediatric surgery at Schneider Children's Hospital of Long Island Jewish Medical Center in New York. Two years after my pull-through surgery, on August 10, 1998, we had our first consultation with him. Dr. Peña ordered tests and determined that eight inches of my colon needed to come out.

On September 27, 1998, Dr. Peña cut me open from the top of my chest to my belly button. He removed the unhealthy section of my colon and reconnected my other parts. The surgery saved my life.

Even before Dr. Peña became an internationally known pediatric surgeon, he knew the tragedy and grief caused by childhood illnesses all too well. Alberto

Peña was born in Mexico City and was the fourth of five children. Three other siblings born before him had died as toddlers from illnesses such as typhoid fever, gastroenteritis, and respiratory infection. His father was an agricultural engineer and worked for the Mexican government. Alberto's mother and father divorced when he was five years old, and his family split up. He went with his mother, and they moved often, forcing him to constantly change schools. Alberto almost dropped out of school when he was young, but he focused and completed high school.

A turning point in Alberto's life came when his two older sisters met two students attending the Military Medical School in Mexico, and they encouraged Alberto to claim a better life for his family and himself by pursuing a medical degree. He joined the army and enrolled in medical school. Dr. Jesús Lozoya, a Mexican military physician, pediatrician, and politician, became his mentor. Dr. Lozoya also had a son who died. His son had been a medical student, and Dr. Lozoya created an award in his honor. In 1961, Dr. Alberto Peña won the award as he graduated as the top student in his class.

Two years later, Dr. Peña started his four-year surgical training at Central Military Hospital, and afterward he went to University Hospital in Ann Arbor, Michigan, to study under Dr. Cameron Haight, who was an expert in esophageal atresia, a birth defect in which part of a baby's esophagus does not develop properly.

Around this time, Dr. Peña's wife gave birth to a son, Gustavo, who was born with biliary atresia, a condition in infants in which the bile ducts outside and inside the liver are scarred and blocked. The condition, if left untreated, leads to liver failure and cirrhosis.[43] Dr. Peña's son didn't look sick when he was born, but as his liver started failing, he became more jaundiced.

Dr. Peña read a chapter about biliary atresia in a medical book written by Dr. Robert Gross, a pediatric surgeon at Boston Children's Hospital. After Dr. Peña discussed what he had read with Dr. Lozoya, who happened to know Dr. Gross, Dr. Lozoya persuaded Dr. Gross to take on Gustavo as a patient. Dr. Lozoya even wrote Dr. Peña a check to pay for their airline tickets to Boston.

Unfortunately, when Dr. Gross opened up Gustavo's stomach, he determined there was nothing that he could do and sewed him back up. He told Dr. Peña and his wife that Gustavo might survive for another nine months. Liver transplants for children were considered experimental at the time, so a transplant wasn't an option. Gutavo lived for nearly five more years, but he was constantly in pain.

According to Dr. Peña, his young son suffered from pneumonia, bleeding, irritability, and fractures because of his fragile bones. Those five years were extremely challenging for Dr. Peña, his wife, and especially his young son. "Gustavo was a sweet boy with a special, sensitive personality. He was small and fragile, yet he was always protective of his two big, strong younger brothers," Dr. Peña wrote.[44] "It is certainly an excruciating pain for parents to see their baby's misery and not be able to help him. Perhaps, it is even more painful to perceive that the child grows and develops his own personality. He becomes aware of his condition and asks many questions—questions that cannot be answered."[45]

That agonizing personal experience and the desire to honor his son inspired Dr. Peña to become a pediatric surgeon. He wished to help other parents avoid suffering the same heartache and grief and vowed to improve the surgical techniques used to treat children with congenital colorectal conditions like me. Even after his personal tragedy, he wanted to serve others to make their lives better.[46]

"Parents sometimes are very angry; they are angry with life because of what's happened to them," Dr. Peña said during an interview in 2008. "They are angry because they are suffering. But if you have been there, you understand what it's all about. Our concerns . . . are nothing compared with the suffering of the parents."[47]

After completing four years of training in general

surgery and another two years of medical pediatrics in Mexico, Dr. Peña wrote a letter to Dr. Gross, informing him that Dr. Peña had decided to become a pediatric surgeon and wanted to study under Dr. Gross. In 1969, Dr. Peña became a research fellow in cardiovascular surgery at Boston Children's Hospital under Dr. Gross and was eventually promoted to a senior resident in surgery.[48]

Gustavo died in December 1969. Dr. Peña and his wife had decided to keep their son out of hospitals, even giving him blood transfusions at home. When Gustavo became very ill shortly before Christmas 1969, he overheard his parents discussing taking him to the hospital. His final words to his father, as Dr. Peña held Gustavo in his arms, were, "Do not take me to the hospital."[49]

Dr. Peña has since written about how Gustavo would have been a candidate for a transplant if he were born today:

I cannot stop thinking what would be better—being born in 1965 and dying young or being born in 2010, enduring the trials of being on the list of transplant recipients (with high chances of dying while waiting), having a liver transplant (with the risk of dying) and a life full of constant medical supervision (always at risk of a rejection). I have no clear answers for those questions but I feel at peace with the way things happened. With everything that occurred at a sensitive stage of my professional life, Gustavo's short life influenced me in an extremely positive way.[50]

While working under Dr. Gross, Dr. Peña learned that his mentor was a man of few words. And, strangely, he seemed to be obsessed with the appearance of the doctors in his program. For example, if a resident's shoes weren't white and clean, Dr. Gross wouldn't talk to him. The doctor simply would get a note from Dr. Gross's assistant, instructing him to clean his shoes.

The story about Dr. Peña and his mentor's obsession with shoes was far different from the lesson of Jesus washing His twelve disciples' feet the evening before His crucifixion. Jesus had instructed Peter and John to prepare their last meal (Luke 22:8), including the unleavened bread that represents His broken body and the wine that signifies His blood when we still take communion today.

During supper, Peter was surprised to see Jesus rise and remove His outer garment and wrap a towel around His waist. Then Jesus filled a basin with water and moved from disciple to disciple, removing their sandals and washing their feet. This was typically a menial task left to servants, not the Messiah. Jesus was showing His disciples that if He was willing to serve in humility, they were obligated to do the same. As Christians, we are supposed to submit to, care for, and serve one another (John 13:1–17).

In 1972, Dr. Peña was lured back to Mexico City to take the role of surgeon-in-chief at the new National Institute of Pediatrics. Eight years later, he revolutionized a new way to approach the surgical repair of anorectal malformations in children like me, and doctors around the world are still using it to improve patients' lives.[51] Dr. Peña has treated thousands of children in dozens of countries, and he has taught his pull-through technique to hundreds of surgeons. Can you think of a better way to serve than saving the life of a child? I know I will forever be grateful to him for making my life so much better.

* * *

What can you do to serve others? While you may not make the kind of impact Dr. Peña has made on the world, there are still things you can do in your daily life that help others. It's as simple as taking your children to build snowmen outside a nursing home during the next snowstorm, picking up lunch for the stranger behind you in the drive-through line, complimenting the first three people you see each day, sending positive text messages to your friends, or leaving behind quarters at the laundromat for someone who might need them. Deliver a meal to someone who lives alone or offer to care for a young couple's children so they can have a date night. Your act of service doesn't need to be difficult or expensive. It only has to be *kind*.

As Christians, we are supposed to submit to, care for, and serve one another.

We admire generous people. Fortunately, anyone can be generous. It's not necessary to be wealthy, talented, skilled, attractive, or even likable to be generous. Anyone is able to give something to others, even if it's just a shoulder to cry on. What you might not realize is how much you gain by being generous to others.

You're not just helping someone else; you're helping yourself too. Being generous has even been shown to add years to your life![52]

Generosity is great for your physical and mental health. Generosity can be free, and it's good for both you and the recipient of your generosity. Give generosity a try and see how it works for you. Make it a policy to perform one act of generosity each day and notice the results. Generosity might become a habit!

Anyone is able to give something to others, even if it's just a shoulder to cry on.

When you grow up in a small community, you realize that helping others isn't something you do—it's just the way you are. Running errands, going to the shop for items missed off the shopping list, helping neighbors with their gardens, or cleaning their cars gives you a sense of belonging and purpose. In this modern, high-speed world, in which it seems hardly anybody knows their neighbors, random acts of kindness are wonderful ways to reconnect with what's really important in life. And they have the most amazing ripple effect! It all starts with a smile and a hello, both of which can be very contagious.

As Dr. Peña showed us, we can inspire others and help those in need even when we have experienced the most unimaginable heartache.

CHAPTER FOUR

Be a Friend

SOME OF MY most cherished memories as a kid are playing hide-and-seek with my cousins at my grandparents' home in Colorado, where we go skiing every winter. Once, when a cousin was trying to find me, an unusual clue gave me away. After smelling an awful odor in the hallway, he heard a giggle coming from the closet. He opened the door, and I popped out trying to scare him. "Aw, man, I ruined the surprise because I had too many beans for lunch," I told him.

Someone with a tremendous sense of humor once suggested that you know you've found true love when you can break wind in front of your significant other.[53] Knowing my father's sophomoric fondness for comedy, I'm pretty sure my mom didn't have to wait very long in their relationship to find out his true feelings for her, if you know what I mean.

Passing gas is a normal function of the human body, and most of us, depending on one's level of maturity, either find flatulence hilariously funny or embarrassingly terrifying. While toots might be viewed as uncouth, the fact is we need to pass gas from time to time. But if a toot is a sign of true love, then I'm pretty sure sitting with your buddy through his hour-long enema has to be the ultimate sign of true friendship.

My closest and oldest friend in the world is Thomas Stevenson, whom I've known since we were toddlers. Thomas and I were born about a month apart (he is older). My dad, Jim, played sports in high school with his father, Tom. Since we were so close in age, my mom became good friends with his mother, Colleen. Our families had dinner together, our parents attended the same Bible studies, and we took vacations together. Our mothers took turns babysitting, and more times than not, we ended up at my house for play-dates because at least once or twice each day, I'd have to head to the bathroom for an hour-long enema to help my body pass solids.

My colostomy bag had

> *If a toot is a sign of true love, then I'm pretty sure sitting with your buddy through his hour-long enema has to be the ultimate sign of true friendship.*

been reversed when I was just over a year old, and by this time my parents had to give me enemas while I was lying on the floor and catheterize me through the anus. It took forever and sometimes didn't work, which meant we had to do it all over again. When I was ten years old I had the Malone procedure, which rerouted everything through my belly button. It was a faster process and not nearly as uncomfortable. In fact, I still have to do it every day.

When I do my bowel treatment, I mix a concoction of glycerin, Dr. Bronner's Pure Castile Soap, and water in an IV bag. The fluids flush me out from top to bottom, through my small intestine, colon, rectum, anus, and eventually into the toilet. It typically takes about thirty to forty minutes, but if my stools are hard and the fluids won't work, it can be a daylong process. On those days, I might start the treatment at seven o'clock in the morning and not finish until four o'clock in the afternoon. It's not much fun, and it wears me down.

It's still better than having to use a colostomy bag, that's for sure. Ask my former babysitter, Sarah Kennedy Gilpin, who started caring for me when I was still using one. At the time, Sarah was only fifteen years old, and she became a member of our family and one of my closest friends. Sarah wanted to be a nurse and loved helping people. Sometimes, if I was playing too hard, the colostomy bag would fall off. On rare occasions, the bag would explode—sometimes all over Sarah! There were a few nights my parents came home to find Sarah wearing Mom's clothes.

Sarah is married now and her daughter, Lauren, is diabetic. Sarah says her time with me helped prepare her for raising a child with diabetes. She says I taught her to be patient and flexible. She appreciated how I overcame the difficult times in life, with little to no complaining, no matter the obstacle. Sarah knows that she and Lauren will get through rough patches, just like I did.

One day, when I was in elementary school, I was playing with my next-door neighbor, Stephen, when Dad yelled that it was time for my enema. I told Stephen goodbye and ran inside. Our phone rang a few minutes later. It was Stephen's mother. "Stephen just asked me when he gets to do his enema," his mother said. Stephen's mother didn't know the full extent of my medical problems. Both parents agreed that Stephen probably wouldn't want one! From that day forward, Dad started calling my enema a "treatment" so it wouldn't confuse my friends.

While the smell and sounds of an enema would gross out most kids and send them running for the hills, my best friend Thomas was patient and simply shrugged it off. He even sat on the bathroom floor waiting for me to finish. Eventually, Mom put a desk in the bathroom for us. I sat on my throne waiting to drop off the kids with a towel over my lap, while Thomas sat at the desk across from me. We played with LEGO blocks, Matchbox cars, PLAYMOBIL toys, and Rescue Heroes action figures to pass the time. Thomas sat right there with me, day after day, and didn't think twice about it.

When it was time for me to finish, Thomas would leave the room. Then we'd pick up where we'd left off. That's the thing I'll always love about Thomas: he never treated me differently because of my differences, never teased me about them, and just never thought much about them.

Thomas and I spent so much time together when we were kids. During the spring and summer, when the weather was nice in Michigan, we built forts and tents on top of the shed behind my house, complete with a pulley system to get everything we needed up there. On any given day we were firefighters or police officers, always fighting the good fight against the bad guys. During the cold winters, we built snow forts or pitched our tents inside.

When my parents purchased the house they're still living in now, Dad gave me one room upstairs to make my own. It was basically a big closet. He said I could decorate it any way I wanted (as long as I kept the door closed). Thomas and I painted the walls, and that became our clubhouse. We even had girlfriends, but I can't remember what they looked like.

In the fourth and fifth grades, Thomas and I played peewee football together for the Grosse Pointe Red Barons. Despite my diminutive size, our coach made me the starting center. Dad had to remind Coach Cimm that I was dyslexic and might forget the snap count. Thomas was the noseguard, so we went head-to-head in practice every day. He wore the number 54 jersey; I wore number 55. Thomas and I also played lacrosse together for the Jays, and even though I was one of the smaller guys on the field, I wasn't afraid to get dirty and scoop up ground balls, which can be dangerous. As you might imagine, even though I was smaller than other kids my age, I didn't back down from anyone. I wasn't frail or anything like that, and my speed and desire compensated for what I lacked in size.

Each summer, Thomas and I left for a week to attend SpringHill camp in Evart, Michigan. It's an interdenominational Christian camp that has been around for more than four decades. We had so much fun there. We played Skittle Skattle Battle in the hills and woods around the camp; it was our own version of tag with snack-sized bags of Skittles, which we hurled about a hundred miles per hour at one another. We went horseback riding and tubing on the lake. There was a rock wall to climb and even a zip line. We played just about every single sport. We were never bored, that's for sure. It was such a wonderful place for kids to spend the summer.

Thomas and I slept in the same cabin at SpringHill, and that's where we talked to the older counselors about faith and read Scripture. Thomas was right next to me the night I professed my faith in Jesus Christ while we were sitting around the campfire. I'd been baptized as a baby and my family went to a church regularly, but as I grew older I began to understand more about my faith, especially given the physical ailments I'd had to endure. I knew I loved Jesus and He had a plan for me, whatever it was.

Another one of my closest friends is Gregory Nelson. As with Thomas's family, Mom and Dad are also close to Gregory's parents. Gregory is more like my brother. He even calls my mother his "mom," and I call his mother my "mom." During the summers, Gregory and I spent many weekends together at the Old Club, which is located on Harsens Island in the Lake St. Clair Flats and is most accessible by boat. It's so close to Canada that you can hit Windsor, Ontario, by skipping a stone.

The Old Club is, as you might guess, very old. It was founded in 1872 by a group of industrialists from Detroit who pitched in $25 each for shares of the Lake St. Clair Fishing and Shooting Club of Detroit. It had a small dock and twenty-six

I knew I loved Jesus and He had a plan for me, whatever it was.

boathouses. Eventually it became a social gathering spot and retreat for many families who built summer homes there. In 1902, it was rechristened as the Old Club, and it remains so more than one hundred years later.[54] We still spend quite a bit of time at the Old Club, boating, fishing, shooting skeet, and swimming in the pool.

One of the best things about living in Grosse Pointe Farms, Michigan, is fishing and boating on Lake St. Clair, which is sometimes referred to as the "sixth Great Lake."[55] It's not nearly as big as the other five, covering only 430 square miles, and isn't nearly as deep. Still, it provides great freshwater fishing and boating. It was an endless playground for me while I was growing up. Gregory and I grew up on the water together. As soon as we could swim, we were spending summer days on the lake fishing for bass, walleye, pike, and muskellunge. Some days, we'd catch a boatload of fish. Other days, we wouldn't catch anything but still had tall fish tales to share. Nowadays, if we're not fishing together, Gregory and I have one rule between us: if there's no photo, there's no proof. We sailed and boated when we were kids, and we still ride Jet Skis together. We're like Maverick and Goose from *Top Gun* on the water.

True friends are authentic and honest. They're your friends when you're around them and when you're not. I have been blessed with so many tremendous friends, not just Thomas and Gregory. We all want to have friends and personal connections in our lives. That has never been more evident than during the pandemic, when so many people have felt alone. We all want to experience the feeling of community, whether we get that through family, friends, coworkers, or others. People make us happy, and if you want people to be around you, then you need to be a happy and kind person. No one wants to be a lone wolf. Reflect on the characteristics of who you want to be and who you want your friends to be. Remember that you are who your friends are, so choose your friends wisely.

Of course, life changes, and we grow up fast. When I went away to college, Gregory attended Michigan State University and Thomas left for Rollins College in Florida. Fortunately, each of us moved back home after graduation, so we see one another quite a bit. Your best friends are the ones who are difficult to find, impossible to leave, and the ones you will never forget. I guess that old Irish proverb about friends is true: a good friend is like

Having close friends gives us people to turn to when we feel lonely, need a listening ear, or want to celebrate.

a four-leaf clover, hard to find and lucky to have. I know I'm the luckiest man in the world.

Although you've most likely created good social relationships over the years, brushing up on our friendship skills can be beneficial for all of us. Having close friends gives us people to turn to when we feel lonely, need a listening ear, or want to celebrate. If you've ever had a really great friend, you've noticed all the things they did with you, for you, and on your behalf.

Whether you're learning to be that kind of a friend yourself or you just want to polish up your "good friend" skills, these ideas might help you establish and maintain positive, fulfilling friendships.

Be a good listener. We all have times when we just want to vent. When you make the decision to listen rather than offer feedback or suggestions, you're practicing one of the most important behaviors a good friend can do. Keep your ears and mind open.

Support your friends. Be someone your friend

can count on. Be dependable and predictable in your friendship. Doing so will ensure that you'll never have a shortage of people who care for you.

Spend time with your friends. Your time is even more valuable than your words. We all lead busy lives, but make a commitment to do something fun, have dinner, paint the living room, work on the car, or just hang out. A good friend wants to be together and makes time in a busy schedule to do it. Be creative in the planning of activities and you'll make great memories.

Being a great friend will bring you moments of joy, years of comfort, and decades of cherished memories. Implement these strategies in your relationships today. You will feel like you're the best friend ever and those you care about will think so too!

CHAPTER FIVE

Find Your Tribe

ONE OF MY DAD'S favorite movies is *Groundhog Day*, in which Bill Murray plays Phil Connors, a cynical TV weatherman who finds himself stuck in the same day over and over again after he goes on assignment to the annual Groundhog Day event in Punxsutawney, Pennsylvania.

After getting stranded in Punxsutawney because of a snowstorm, Murray's character wakes up each morning on February 2, 1992, waiting to find out if the groundhog Punxsutawney Phil is going to see his shadow or not. No matter what Phil Connors does, he keeps reliving the same day.

Michelle Philpots, a woman in her late fifties from Spalding, England, is a real-life version of Murray's movie character. Shortly after meeting her husband, Michelle was involved in a bad motorcycle accident. Then in 1990, she was in a car wreck that left her with serious head injuries. She suffered seizures that damaged her brain and led to short-term memory loss.

Each day, Michelle wakes up and doesn't remember that she is married; her husband uses a photo album to remind her of their wedding day. Michelle remembers everything that happened in her life before the accidents, yet she can't recall what she did yesterday or even a few hours earlier. Michelle wakes up every morning believing it's 1994.[56]

A neuroscience specialist at Cambridge University, Dr. Peter Nestor, said that Philpots suffers from anterograde amnesia, which causes people to lose the ability to make and recall new memories. While long-term memories remain, a person's short-term memory disappears.[57]

"It is reasonably rare but it does exist," Dr. Nestor said in 2010. "You are capable of carrying out day-to-day things and don't forget how to do certain things like speaking. But if someone was to ask you what you did yesterday, you wouldn't have a clue."[58]

It's the same kind of amnesia the blue tang fish Dory has in the Disney movies *Finding Nemo* and *Finding Dory*. Dory is able to recall memories of her parents and where they lived when she was a child. However, she can't remember more recent facts like Nemo's name or exactly where she is going.

I know how Dory feels. Shortly after I turned five years old, I was enrolled in the Montessori Early School at Grosse Pointe Academy in Grosse Pointe Farms, Michigan. One afternoon, while Mom and I waited in the long carpool line after school, she began pointing out my classmates and asking me their names. No matter how hard I tried, I couldn't remember them. I couldn't even remember my teacher's name.

At home, I couldn't recall the words to simple songs we had been singing in class, and I didn't remember the alphabet, even though Mom and I had been reciting it together for months. Mom and I read the poem "Jack and Jill" over and over again at bedtime. But when she'd ask me about the poem we'd just read, I only remembered that Jack and Jill went up the hill—not that Jack fell down and Jill came tumbling after.[59] It was the same scenario with "Humpty Dumpty." I remembered that he sat on a wall, yet not that all the king's horses and all the king's men couldn't put Humpty together again.[60]

When Mom and Dad approached my preschool teacher about their concerns, she brushed my poor memory off as absentmindedness and nothing to be too concerned about. My ability to remember names and facts didn't improve over the next few months, however, so Mom and Dad scheduled a conference with the head of the school. After several meetings, he suggested that maybe Montessori Early School wasn't the right place for me. My parents have always been my biggest advocates, and they were going to do everything in their power to put me in the best academic environment. I know God blessed me with loving and supportive parents and an extended family who opened their arms to me. Not everyone is blessed to have a support system like that.

That is why it is imperative to find your tribe,

whether it's family, friends, coworkers, or simply people who have the same interests as you. We can't do life alone, but we have to remember that the tribe we might want isn't always the one we need. Write down the names of three people you might want to be friends with. Reflect on their strengths and weaknesses. Do they have the same characteristics you want people to recognize in you? If not, find someone else to be in your tribe. The pursuit of your tribe never ends. I know that was certainly the case for me as we searched for teachers, tutors, specialists, and doctors who could help me learn to read and write.

After preschool, I transferred to another school, University Liggett School in Grosse Pointe Woods, which is the oldest independent coeducational school in Michigan.[61] Within the first few weeks of classes there, my first-grade teacher, Peggy Dettlinger, recognized the same alarming signs my parents had noticed. I wasn't acting out and was following her instructions. I paid attention in class as much

We can't do life alone, but we have to remember that the tribe we might want isn't always the one we need.

as any six-year-old kid could. Yet I was struggling to complete my work. Over the next few months, my learning differences stumped Mrs. Dettlinger and other teachers at University Liggett School.

My parents recognized other problems at home. I was not only struggling to remember letters but, also couldn't remember numbers well. I couldn't memorize our home phone number, address, or even 911. As difficult as reading was for me, I struggled with math because I couldn't recall the symbols for addition, subtraction, division, and multiplication. I forgot the signs that identified the men's and women's restrooms at restaurants and school. That was embarrassing!

I loved banging on my keyboard as a kid, but when my parents signed me up for piano lessons, it was a lost cause because I couldn't remember the notes, let alone read sheet music. The same was true of dance classes; I couldn't remember the steps. I loved sports, and I played football, lacrosse, and just about everything else. But my parents couldn't figure out why I disliked taekwondo so much. It took them more than a year to discern that I couldn't remember to bow to my instructors and opponents, how to sit inside the dojang, or any of the other rituals that are associated with this martial art.

It wasn't as if I had amnesia like Michelle Philpots. I recognized my parents, my dog, Duke, my friends,

Something was misfiring in my brain, which wasn't allowing me to learn how to read and write or to memorize letters, numbers, and symbols.

and my grandparents. I hadn't forgotten who they were or the events that had shaped my life up to that point. I could remember what I'd done at school that day and what I'd eaten for dinner the night before.

When it came to anything I read, though, I forgot the material only a short time later. It was like my brain didn't absorb what my eyes were reading. In many ways, I felt like Phil Connors in *Groundhog Day* because I started each day as I had every day before—I couldn't read and write.

Finally, in the spring of 2003, University Liggett School referred my parents to Dr. Marquita Bedway, a well-respected educational psychologist. She put me through a battery of tests, observed me in the classroom, and interviewed my parents and teachers. In her final report, Dr. Bedway determined that my general cognitive ability was in the high average range of intellectual functioning, and my nonverbal reasoning abilities were superior. However, something was misfiring in my brain, which wasn't allowing me to learn how to read and write or to memorize letters, numbers, and symbols. She wrote in her final report:

> JT's abilities to sustain attention, concentration, and exert mental control are a weakness relative to his verbal reasoning abilities. Mental control is the ability to attend to and hold information in a short-term memory while performing some operation or manipulation with it. A weakness in mental control may make the processing of complex information more time consuming for JT, drain his mental energies more quickly as compared to other children his age.

Basically, what Dr. Bedway determined was that my functional IQ was 115, which doctors consider superior intelligence and high, but not higher than most other people. When it came to reading, spelling, and mathematics, however, my scores were borderline or low average. I simply couldn't remember words, numbers, or symbols because of short-term memory loss.

In December 2003, the Grosse Pointe Public

School System agreed to evaluate my needs for special services. The Individuals with Disabilities Education Act requires public schools to create an individualized education program (IEP) for any child with learning differences, even students attending private schools in the district. The evaluation confirmed Dr. Bedway's assessment and what my parents and teachers already knew: my educational achievement was very low. My very first IEP included preferential seating, modified assignments, oral testing, and longer time for tests. Those were the only things the district recommended at the time.

Unless you've struggled to learn to read, you don't know how painful the learning process can be. I recognized letters while trying to read, but I couldn't remember the sounds the letters made. Once I mastered the phonetics of the alphabet, I struggled to put letters together to build words or put words together to construct sentences. Even after I learned to read, which was a long and arduous process (more on that in the next chapter), I still struggled to remember what I'd just read because of my short-term memory loss. While I might have grabbed onto one theme or fact in the passage, I'd forget the rest of it.

It's the same way with video games. When I was younger, I spent hours playing *Madden NFL*, *Call of Duty*, *Forza Motorsport*, and other video games with my friends. My buddies probably loved playing *Madden NFL* against me because I couldn't remember what play I had selected only a few minutes earlier, which typically led to a turnover or busted assignment. I could tell you that I was playing with the Detroit Lions because of their blue-and-silver uniforms, but I couldn't remember that Matthew Stafford was the quarterback or Calvin Johnson was a receiver. Even reading words like *start*, *exit*, and *pause* on the TV was a challenge.

My lack of short-term memory is one of the reasons we never played many board games as a family. Kids' games like Concentration, Memory, and other card games were too frustrating for me. Sometimes, when I'm at a friend's house for the holidays, I'll sit back and watch my friends play games instead of actively participating because it's too difficult for me to remember the instructions. On several occasions, friends have asked me to team up with them to keep me involved so I don't feel left out.

I guess one of the good things about having poor short-term memory is that I've never been much of a gambler. In a card game like blackjack, I can't remember that an ace is worth one or eleven or that face cards are worth ten. Las Vegas would absolutely love if I bellied up to a table from time to time!

When Mom sends me to the grocery store to pick up a few things, she makes sure to write a list. Without one, I'll usually come home without at least one thing she wanted. That happens to all of us from time to time, but it happens to me more often than not if I don't take a list.

What my family and I have learned over the years is that my memory is much better if I've experienced and visualized something. Even though I might not remember the names of streets or places, I can remember how to get somewhere familiar. When we were driving to northern Michigan to go boating in the summer or skiing in the winter, I'd often remind my parents about an upcoming turn or exit. If a friend calls and asks me to meet them for lunch, I might not remember the name of a particular restaurant, but I might know that it was a brunch place across the street from a park or a coffee shop near the library. I can tell you most of the intimate details about family vacations and other events because I experienced them and lived them.

Here's a specific example: many years ago, when I was probably a freshman in high school, I was at the Grosse Pointe Yacht Club on the same day one of my parents' friends, Dr. Dave Martin, was celebrating his birthday. Dr. Martin, a cardiologist, invited me to have lunch at his table, and then I invited him to take a boat ride on Lake St. Clair and the Detroit River. During that ride, United States Coast Guard officers pulled us over for a random check of life vests, registration, and other safety verifications.

When one of the officers addressed Dr. Martin like he was the boat's captain, he pointed at me and said, "He's the captain." When the officers wanted to check the inboard engines, I had to explain to them that the boat only had outboard motors, which made me giggle. Anyhow, about ten years later, for whatever reason, I remembered Dr. Martin's birthday. I sent him a text message, wishing him a happy birthday and a great day.

Dr. Martin said he probably received twenty voicemails and seventy text messages on his birthday, but mine meant the most because he couldn't figure out how I'd remembered that it was his birthday. He called my mother the next day and asked if she'd put me up to it. The only thing I can figure is that I remembered the date because we had taken the boat ride together, so I'd experienced the event.

Of course, my short-term memory loss was much more of a concern when I was a kid. My parents and teachers had to come up with a plan to attack the problem. I wanted to learn to read and write more than anything. Even though I wasn't nearly as good of a reader as the other children in my class, I was still eager to learn. At first, I was nervous about reading in front of my classmates. Fortunately, most of them encouraged me despite my struggles.

In the third grade, I routinely held up my hand when my teacher, Linda Brown, asked someone to read from a book. Each time, she picked someone else. One day, Mrs. Brown told me that we were going to practice a sentence together and then she would call on me the next day. When she did, I read the sentence perfectly. One of the girls in my class started clapping for me. Soon everyone in the class was cheering me on. All these years later, I still remember how proud that moment made me feel. That's what kindness does for someone.

In 2005, two years after the Grosse Pointe Public School System established an IEP program to help me learn, administrators called my parents to an annual meeting. The head of the University Liggett Lower School was there, along with a special education teacher and my teachers from the third and fourth grades. A learning specialist, speech patholo-gist, district representative, and school psycholo-gist also attended the meeting.

Over the previous several months, my parents had tried everything to help me learn to read and write, including specialized reading programs, tutors, and much prayer. Students in my classes were already reading chapter books while I was still struggling to spell and read simple words. No matter what my parents and I tried, nothing seemed to work.

During the meeting, the Grosse Pointe Public School psychologist summarized the results of my testing and shared what she had observed while visiting my classroom. Then she abruptly stopped. My parents will always remember what she said next: "Mr. and Mrs. Mestdagh, it's my conclusion that JT is illiterate and always will be. He will never learn to read. You as a family need to accept that and learn how to cope going forward."

Tears filled my parents' eyes as the psychologist hurriedly suggested a few special schools for students like me. Then Dad interrupted her.

"JT will learn to read," he said. "We will find a way to help him learn to read."

And with that, the meeting was over.

One of the more poignant scenes in *Finding Dory* is when Dory says, "I can remember some things because, well, uh, they make sense. Like, I have a family . . . everyone has a family."[62]

Despite struggling to remember many things, Dory never forgets that she has a family out there somewhere in the deep blue sea. If nothing else, she remembers that her parents love her and she

Family is God's greatest blessing to us, and family is the anchor that holds us through life's storms.

loves them. Family is God's greatest blessing to us, and family is the anchor that holds us through life's storms.

My parents waited several years to share the details of that meeting with me. By that time, I already knew that they were never going to give up on me. That's something I would never forget.

CHAPTER SIX

Take Off Your Mask

(No, Not That One)

....

IF YOU'RE ANYTHING like me, you probably got sick and tired of having to wear a mask in public during the pandemic. Scientists discovered that wearing masks helped slow the spread of COVID-19,[63] so we had to cover our faces in any situation in which we couldn't stay six feet apart from other people, whether we went to the grocery store, ate in a restaurant, sat in class, or rode on public transportation. If anything, I think masks probably revealed to all of us how truly terrible our own morning breath is.

* * *

Being real and original isn't easy, and you have to take off your mask to do it—which is downright scary and uncomfortable. It requires bold courage and strength to take off a mask. Believe me, I know what it's like.

In 2006, I was in the fifth grade. I still couldn't read and write. When I was a kid, my mother documented my medical and education journeys in myriad journals and notes. Around this time, Mom

Being real and original isn't easy, and you have to take off your mask to do it—which is downright scary and uncomfortable.

wrote: "In school since the beginning, JT has struggled and continues to do so. His memory is an issue also. One teacher said it is like a 'stroke victim.' He has the info, but he can't retrieve it. Another teacher, Mrs. [Peggy] Dettlinger, felt JT's mind is like a light switch; one day it is on, and one day it is off."

Unfortunately, the switch was off most of the time. It felt like someone had flipped the circuit breaker to my brain. We needed to find someone who could help us switch it back on and leave it there. A family friend, Kathy Genthe, had children who struggled with learning differences and introduced my parents to a man named Steve Tattum. Steve studied special education at Eastern Illinois University and George Washington University. He was a director of the Denver Academy, a private day school in Denver, Colorado, where he developed the radical but highly successful F.A.S.T. Reading System (now called Tattum Reading).[64]

Kathy and her husband, Richard, had tried myriad for-profit reading systems with their children and felt frustrated with the education system before their family started working with Steve. The F.A.S.T. Reading System had made a world of difference.

When my parents reached out to Steve, he just so happened to be in Detroit training teachers in his program. So one night in September 2006, we drove to meet Steve at a hotel in Bloomfield Hills, Michigan. When we arrived at the hotel, Steve was sitting alone in a dimly lit lobby. He had shaggy gray-blond hair and a mustache.

Steve shook hands with Mom and Dad and then he dropped to one knee and looked me in the eye. "And you must be JT. Let's get started, okay?"

As Steve walked me down a hallway to a conference room he was using as his office that week, I could feel the pit in my stomach. Would this appointment be another worthless meeting with another educator who would come to the same conclusion as everyone else? Were my hopes and dreams going to be dashed once again? Would I ever learn to read and write?

On the table between us, Steve placed a flip-book. It looked exactly like all the flip-books I'd used in every other unsuccessful reading program before this one. It was made of card stock with spiral binding and had tabs of letters in bright colors. Steve used the letters to spell out simple words like *bat*, *cat*, *den*, and *pen*. I felt my anxiety rise as I unsuccessfully tried to read them. As Steve cleaned up the way I pronounced consonants and vowels, I tried to read words for about ten minutes without any luck.

I'll never forget what Steve did next: he flung the flip-book across the room. "You'll never see that again," he promised me. I knew right then that Steve was different from anyone else I'd worked with before. I could trust him.

Steve pulled out a rectangular whiteboard about the size of a laptop. It had small magnetic tiles of letters scattered all over it. It looked like a Scrabble board filled with jumbled words. For a few minutes, we went through what Steve called the vowel galaxy. Then he flipped over the board.

The other side was covered with tiles made up of two to four letters like *un*, *ex*, *rupt*, *mit*, *ble*, and *tion*—organized in colors. Steve used them to spell out a word I'd never seen before. "Okay, JT. Read that one," he said.

"Un . . . rupt . . . tion," I said. "What's that mean?"

"It's a nonsense word," he told me. "But did you see what you just did? You just read a three-syllable word."

We went over "words" like *un-rupt-tion* for thirty minutes or so. Then Steve handed me one of his books called *Ocean Fun*. He asked me to read a sentence that most first graders could conquer: "It's fun in the sun." I made two mistakes, and Steve corrected me. He read the next two sentences. We went on like that for a page and a half. Before too long, I realized that I was reading!

In that first meeting, Steve accomplished what every educator before him had failed to do: he instilled in me the confidence that I could read. Because of my short-term memory problems and processing disorder, I had one of the worst cases of dyslexia Steve had ever encountered in his thirty years working with children who have learning differences.

What made me different from other students who struggled to read, however, was that I didn't use a mask to hide the problem. I cared and desperately wanted to learn to read and write, no matter how hard I had to work and how vulnerable and exposed I felt. Sure, I was nervous and didn't want to be laughed at or ridiculed by other kids because I couldn't read and write as well as them. Even sitting there with Steve, who was a stranger, I was nervous and uncomfortable. But my desire to learn was stronger than my feelings, so I didn't pretend to be something I wasn't.

Unlike other kids, I didn't mask my learning differences by not trying hard enough or not applying myself. All too often, this is what happens: instead of

I cared and desperately wanted to learn to read and write, no matter how hard I had to work and how vulnerable and exposed I felt.

confronting the problem and working through it, kids who are struggling to learn simply stop caring and give up. They might sit in the back row of class instead of being engaged and never raise their hands. They also might act out and become defiant to mask their learning differences.

But even though I wasn't doing any of those things, the process of learning was still not a fun experience for me. That is, until I met Steve. I was so excited leaving that first meeting. A door in my brain that had previously been closed suddenly opened. On the drive home that night, my parents were amazed as I sounded out the names on street signs. I spent a week working with Steve before he went back to Colorado. After only a few days, one of my teachers called Mom.

"What are you doing with JT?" she asked.

"What do you mean?" Mom replied.

The teacher had handed out a homework

assignment and expected to have to explain to me what I was supposed to be reading. But when she came to my desk to collect my work, she was amazed that I had already answered the questions.

"Kris, he had already filled out the worksheet! I asked him how, and he said, 'I read it!' Kris, what's going on?" my teacher asked.

Steve said I was the most motivated child he had ever encountered. I wanted to read. Each night, before I went to bed, I prayed to God to allow me to read. Each year, my birthday wish was to be able to read and write.

Steve's system gave me the confidence to do it. Suddenly, I had self-esteem. The anxiety and dread about learning to read, which I'd had for so long, were gone. I was no longer intimidated when a teacher called on me. My hands no longer sweated during tests. I was certain I could do the work.

When Steve returned to Colorado, my parents arranged for me to continue working with a F.A.S.T. tutor named Susie Jacobs. I'd go to my classes at University Liggett School until three o'clock, and then Mom would drive me forty-five minutes to Farmington Hills, Michigan, to work with Mrs. Susie and Deb North, another tutor who helped me with homework. After that, I'd go home for my hour-long bowel "treatment," followed by more homework and dinner, before finally going to bed.

Steve had advised my parents that I might benefit from enrolling at the Denver Academy, where I could continue to work with him. Dad couldn't move to Colorado because of work, and my parents didn't want to be separated for so long. Sending me off as a boarding student wasn't an option, either, because of my medical issues. Since I was making good progress with the F.A.S.T. tutors, Mom and Dad decided we should continue down that road, as exhausting as it was for us with all the driving back and forth.

Then everything suddenly changed.

Just before Thanksgiving break during the fifth grade, I was walking down the hall at school when I heard a man say, "JT! Got a minute?"

It was the headmaster of University Liggett School. He motioned me over to a corner near the water fountain. He had his golden retriever with him; he brought the dog to school nearly every day. I was looking down at his dog when he delivered the devastating news.

"JT, I need to let you know that you're not reading or writing well enough for you to stay at Liggett for middle school," the headmaster told me. "You can't come here next year."

I couldn't believe what I'd heard. He had ambushed me with the news right before the holiday. Even if it hadn't been a holiday, what kind of man says *that* to an eleven-year-old child? I knew he hadn't informed my parents yet because they would have broken the news to me gently. Let me tell you, at that moment, I wished I had a mask so I could hide how much his words truly hurt me.

"Yes, sir," was all I could muster before I walked slowly out the school's back door. I ran through the grassy area that separated the campus from my backyard. By the time I ran through the side door of my house, I was crying uncontrollably. The only thought in my head was that I was stupid.

Mom quickly grabbed me and examined me up and down for injuries.

"JT! What happened? What's wrong?" she asked.

I was crying so hard that I couldn't answer her.

Finally, I calmed down enough to tell her about my conversation with the headmaster in the hall. She wanted to march over to the school and confront him right then, but she called Dad instead. My parents scheduled a meeting with the headmaster for the next day, but he didn't show. He sent the headmaster of the lower school instead, who told my parents that the decision had already been made. I wasn't invited back to the school for the next year. I was being banished.

So over that Christmas break, I visited the Denver Academy with Mom and Dad. The teachers and students made me feel like it was where I truly belonged. We located an apartment and rented furniture. In January 2007, Mom and I, along with my dog, Duke, moved to Denver. Dad visited every other weekend and whenever he could get away from work.

One of the first things that I realized about the Denver Academy was that each student there had some sort of learning difference. I'd found a place where I fit in. After only a few weeks, I told Mom, "I don't feel different here. Everyone is like me." No masks needed here!

After only five months of working with Steve, his assistant, Rosemarie Offenhauer (or Mrs. O, as I called her), and the other wonderful teachers and tutors at the Denver Academy, I learned to read and write. I spent each morning working with Steve and Mrs. O in the F.A.S.T. House before joining my classmates.

During a meeting with Mom and Dad, Steve wanted to document my progress in a video. He asked me about my time at the Denver Academy. "It is going great," I told him. "I can read, I can write, and I feel good about myself."

After that meeting, Mrs. O delivered my latest testing results: "You've not only moved up past the first-grade level, the second-grade level, and the third-grade level," she said. "You're reading close to what a typical fifth grader would read. Not only that, you're writing four or five sentences all by yourself."

I was reading and writing, but I hadn't yet

mastered those skills. It's something I'm still working on today. I wrote the following in one of my diaries from March 2007:

> Last night I drove to Beavear Creek. The next day my gramp drove me to ski and snowboard club in Vail. I had a lot of fun on the race cors. My dad came to pick me up. The next day we went to the air port. We wher going to Cinnatti children hospital. Ower plane was dulade for fur hour. We got to our hotel at midnight.

As you can see, my writing wasn't perfect, but it was remarkable progress from where I'd started!

In April 2007, we flew back to Detroit, and my parents met with administrators and teachers at University Liggett School to discuss whether I could return for middle school the next year. They shared my test results and the impressive progress I'd made while working with Steve and attending the Denver Academy. My parents got absolutely no response from the teachers. The headmaster, who had confronted me in the hallway before Thanksgiving, was a no-show at the meeting once again. My parents were told that because of my learning differences, I didn't fit in with the culture at University Liggett and couldn't return there.

During that earlier meeting with Steve and my

parents in Denver, the one that had been filmed, I shared something that had been weighing on my heart for a while: "My only concern is that all the other children in Michigan who struggle with reading may never get to know about F.A.S.T."

My parents made it their mission to help me bring the F.A.S.T. program to schools in Michigan to help kids with learning differences learn to read and write. Mom and Dad made numerous phone calls and sent emails to anyone they knew in the local school systems.

On April 23, 2007, I stood in front of the whiteboard in the field house at Grosse Pointe Academy. I scanned the room of more than one hundred adults and recognized teachers, tutors, principals, and psychologists who had worked with me in the past. A few of them had been the ones who told my parents that I was illiterate for life and would never be able to learn to read and write.

After my father made a few remarks, Steve walked to the dais. He took a few minutes to explain who he was and what the F.A.S.T. Reading System was about. Then he called me up. "Let's show people how much you've learned, okay?" he said.

Steve put me through a full lesson, using the magnetic whiteboard just like we did each morning at the F.A.S.T. House in Denver. At only ten years old, I had removed my mask and was willing to reveal the biggest insecurity in my life. I mustered the strength and courage to show the naysayers how wrong they had been. I'd never felt so exposed.

After the lesson, Steve pulled out his book, *French Quarter Phantom*, which he'd written for middle third- and beginning fourth-grade readers as part of his Moonlight Tales series.[65] I read from the book for about ten minutes. I stumbled a few times but showed the group how much I'd improved over the previous four months.

When the meeting was over, a woman from the audience approached us. I remembered her as someone who had worked with me when I was younger.

"I'm sorry," she said. "But I find it so hard to believe that JT can read like this. I worked with him. I know where he was as a reader just months ago."

I looked at my parents. Mom looked stunned that the woman was suggesting that I couldn't read and that Steve and I had simply memorized the sentences from the book.

Steve was calm and simply asked the woman if she had a piece of paper with writing in her purse. She rummaged through her bag and handed him a sales receipt. He glanced at it and handed it to me. "Read it," Steve told me.

I squinted while trying to make out the small type. "Fresh Farms Market . . . cheddar cheese," I said, before moving down the receipt.

I looked up at Mom and Steve. They had wide smiles on their faces. I knew they were proud of me. The woman was smiling with tears in her eyes. After working with me for so long, she simply couldn't believe it was true.

What are your insecurities? What makes you vulnerable? Why are you wearing a mask? Remember that you need not be physically handicapped to feel handicapped. If you're living a false life by hiding behind a mask, you're limiting yourself. It's a false reality.

* * *

Sooner or later a question shows up in your mind that you just can't answer. You may dismiss it many times, but it'll keep coming back. It's like a stone in your shoe. First, it's just an irritation, but left unanswered, it becomes a blister. And pretty soon, you have an infection. The question that we all face at some point is this: *Is this what life is all about for me? Surely there's more than this! Where have I gone wrong? What can I do? I don't want my life to be like this.*

We've all had it. Frustration, anxiety, lack of fulfillment, doubt, and indecision. They all seem to show up with monotonous regularity, don't they? And they will continue to show up until you change something. When you get right down to it, what most people want is to live peaceful, happy lives and make more money than they need to spend each month. That's all. Then they could spend time with the people they care about and do the things that make their hearts sing.

In other words, they want to live authentically. Authenticity is the inevitable outcome when what you think, what you say, and what you do are in harmony. In fact, it's the only possible outcome. How different would your life be if you woke up each morning with a smile on your face, jumped out of bed, and couldn't wait to start the day? Like when you were a kid and the fair was in town, remember?

Every person, place, or activity that doesn't make you happy is like a rock that you put in your backpack when you go on a hiking trip. You don't have to go far before the extra weight begins to slow you down. Soon every day becomes a chore, and the backpack becomes too heavy to lift. You wonder why life is tough? It's time to unload that backpack!

What happens when you start living authentically? You find yourself smiling during the day for no reason at all. Life suddenly feels lighter. You feel totally capable of letting go of thoughts you neither want nor need. For the first time in a long time, you begin to experience joy. You notice that, without any conscious effort on your part, you have no attachment to the people, places, or things that no longer serve you. Letting them all go becomes effortless.

Living authentically becomes easy. You make

Authenticity is the inevitable outcome when what you think, what you say, and what you do are in harmony. In fact, it's the only possible outcome.

new friends. New people start to come into your life who are in alignment with your new, fresh way of thinking. You have new adventures. Opportunities to experience new activities present themselves, and you find that you're excited to try them. You learn and discover. Your interest in learning new things and acquiring new skills awakens.

Once you start living authentically, your frustration, anxiety, and doubt are replaced with optimism, enthusiasm, and fulfillment in all that you do. Life seems simpler. The sun seems to shine more. Others say you look different, more radiant, and more alive. You are different.

It all begins when you make that decision to let go of everyone and everything that no longer serves you. Take off the mask and live authentically. The change can be dramatic. The feelings are permanent. Try it for yourself. You'll be glad you did!

CHAPTER SEVEN

Pull Off the Label

....

WHEN I WAS younger, my maternal grandparents, John and Marlene Boll, liked to host annual family meetings at the Grosse Pointe Yacht Club on Lake St. Clair. The purpose of the meetings was twofold: it was a great way to get their family together in the middle of the summer, and it was also a time for their grandchildren to share what they had accomplished the previous year with the rest of the family.

My grandparents grew up during the Depression and didn't have an opportunity to attend college. That didn't stop them from building a very successful business from the ground up. They've worked hard to promote the qualities of hard work and education in each of their eight grandchildren, and every year they ask each of us to set goals for the next twelve months.

Some years, they take us to lunch individually to discuss what we have accomplished. In other years, they host formal family meetings so everyone can share what they've done.

In the summer of 2007, after I'd spent five months working with Steve Tattum and the other teachers and tutors at the Denver Academy, I put on my blue blazer and best tie; I couldn't wait to attend the family meeting. I was so excited to share the news that I could read and write. Once everyone took a seat at the large table in the Commodore's Room, Papi stood and asked, "So, kids, what have you been proud of this year?"

I threw up my hand before anyone else. I was sitting to Papi's right, and he turned toward me and smiled.

"One of my goals this year was to learn to read, and I did!" I told everyone with a wide smile on my face.

After I made my announcement, no one in the room said anything. Even my parents were surprised because I hadn't told them what I was going to say. Finally, one of my cousins nervously asked, "What?"

Suddenly, it hit me. My cousins, grandparents, aunts, and uncles hadn't known that I couldn't read and write. They were well aware of my medical problems and knew that I'd struggled in school, but they weren't privy to the intimate details of my learning differences.

"Tell 'em, J," Dad said to me.

"Well, you all know I went to a new school in the winter and spring in Denver, right?" I explained. "When I started there, I could barely make out words most kindergarteners know. Now I can read at a fifth-grade level!"

Later, Papi told my parents that he hadn't known the severity of my learning differences. He didn't want to admit it in front of the rest of his grandkids. "The truth of the matter is, all the cousins assumed he could read," Papi said.

My parents hadn't deliberately hid anything from them. They were just always ones to focus on the positives and plow ahead. Besides, they didn't want others labeling me as illiterate, stupid, or something worse. They knew how mean kids can be.

People like to label others—a lot. . . . It's the labels people use to pass judgment on others that are hurtful.

People like to label others—a lot. We have labels for everything, based on someone's age, sex, ethnicity, political affiliation, religion, or where they live. Labels like Democrat, Republican, Southerner, Northerner, Christian, atheist, Black, white, and Hispanic aren't harmful. Those are descriptions we use to fit people into tidy groups to organize our lives.

It's the labels people use to pass judgment on others that are hurtful. Those labels are based on assumptions and perceptions. They use stereotypes to describe others. I'm sure you know what labels I'm talking about. The ones such as:

- needy
- slow
- jerk
- loser
- ugly
- worthless
- lazy
- fat
- boring

You get the picture. How would you like to be labeled as someone who would never be able to read and write? That's what an administrator and others at my school said about me in the fifth grade. Looking back, I can't believe that adults would put such narrow parameters on a ten-year-old. They simply wanted to give up on me. They wanted my parents and me to stop fighting. They wanted to label me as illiterate and a failure, even when I had my entire life in front of me.

That's the lasting damage that labels can have. Fortunately, my parents refused to accept such a short-sighted assessment and never gave up on me. They continued to fight for me and found the best schools and tutors to help me. What about the other children with learning differences who might not have such supportive parents or the financial resources to go to a wonderful school like the Denver Academy? How much have the labels of being "dumb," a "failure," or an "underachiever" held them back? How different could their lives be?

Let me ask you this: What if legendary novelist F. Scott Fitzgerald had never learned to read because of his dyslexia?[66] What if the American industrialist Henry Ford, who also had dyslexia, had simply given up?[67] Or what if teachers had given up on film director Steven Spielberg because of his learning differences?[68] We never would have been able to read *The Great Gatsby*, drive a Ford F-150, or watch *Jurassic Park* or *Saving Private Ryan*.

There are so many people out there with learning differences whom others have unfairly labeled. According to the International Dyslexia Association, about one-half of students in the United States who qualify for special education are classified as having a learning disability.[69] There are thirteen categories covered under the Individuals with Disabilities Education Act (IDEA), including attention deficit, autism, anxiety, depression, stuttering, and blindness.[70] About 85 percent of those students have a learning difference in reading and language processing.[71] The International Dyslexia Association estimates that as much as 15 to 20 percent of the US population has some form of dyslexia, "including slow or inaccurate reading, poor spelling, poor writing, or mixing up similar words."[72]

The International Dyslexia Association website says, "Dyslexia occurs in people of all backgrounds and intellectual levels" and that "people with dyslexia can be very bright." In fact, "they are often capable or even gifted in areas such as art, computer science, design, drama, electronics, math, mechanics, music, physics, sales, and sports."[73]

You won't believe the list of famous people who struggled in school and were diagnosed with dyslexia or other learning differences. They include inventors, scientists, political leaders, athletes, artists, actors and actresses, military heroes, journalists, filmmakers, and writers. Each one of them overcame adversity and impacted the world in remarkable ways. Here are just a few of those great achievers:

- Muhammad Ali
- Richard Branson
- Albert Einstein
- Magic Johnson
- George S. Patton
- Pablo Picasso
- Nelson Rockefeller
- Charles Schwab
- Ted Turner

The list of people who overcame learning differences also includes Daniel Radcliffe, the actor who played Harry Potter in the famous series. He has a mild form of dyspraxia, which is a neurological order that affects a person's ability to plan and process motor tasks. People with dyspraxia have problems completing physical tasks like tying their shoes, climbing stairs, kicking a ball, jumping, or even sitting down in a chair. In other words, dyspraxia causes clumsiness, which was one of the characteristics of his famous character. Now in his thirties, Radcliffe struggles with his handwriting because of the condition, according to his publicist.

The National Center for Learning Disabilities in New York estimates about 6 percent of all children have some form of dyspraxia, and about 70 percent of them are boys.[74]

In a Q&A with the *Wall Street Journal* in 2014, Radcliffe offered this wonderful advice to young people suffering from dyspraxia: "Do not let it stop you. It has never held me back, and some of the smartest people I know are people who have learning disabilities. The fact that some things are more of a struggle will only make you more determined, harder working and more imaginative in the solutions you find to problems."[75] I couldn't have said it better myself.

Tim Tebow won the Heisman Trophy as the best

college football player in the country at the University Florida in 2007 and helped the Gators win two national championships.[76] After college, he was an NFL quarterback and a professional baseball player with the New York Mets. Tebow was diagnosed with dyslexia when he was seven years old.

Dyslexia runs in his family, he told the *New York Post* during an interview in 2012. His father, Bob, and brother Robby are also dyslexic. His mother, Pamela, homeschooled Tim and his siblings.[77]

Like me, Tim Tebow is a kinesthetic learner and retains information best by doing things and writing lessons down rather than reading textbooks or listening to lectures. He graduated from the University of Florida with a 3.7 GPA.[78] He never let his learning differences stop him from becoming one of the most famous athletes in the world, a man who is as appreciated as much for his faith and kindness as his exploits on the football field and baseball diamond. Most recently, he has worked as a college football analyst for ESPN and the SEC Network.

"There's a lot of people that have certain processing disabilities and it has nothing to do with your intelligence, which I think is a big misconception that people have," Tebow told the *Post.* "I've always tried to share, especially with kids, to be confident with it. You know, 'Hey, this isn't something that's a handicap. You just have to learn how you learn and overcome it. It's something that you can be better off because of, because you know how you learn.'"

What does he think about labeling people?

"When kids get labeled as a dyslexic, they think, 'Oh man, does this make me dumb?'" he said. "'Does this make me stupid? Does this make me not as intelligent as this person?' Absolutely not."[79]

You might know Barbara Corcoran from the hit TV series *Shark Tank*; she overcame dyslexia to launch one of the most successful businesses in the world. Corcoran took a $1,000 loan from her boyfriend, formed her own real estate company in New York, and then sold it for $66 million in 2001. She did all of that despite being a self- described straight-D student in high

"Hey, this isn't something that's a handicap. You just have to learn how you learn and overcome it. It's something that you can be better off be- cause . . . you know how you learn."

—TIM TEBOW

school.[80] She didn't know she had dyslexia until doctors diagnosed her son with the condition.[81]

Corcoran recalls being told by a second-grade teacher that she would always be perceived as stupid until she learned to read. Boy, does that sound familiar. "My burning desire to prove that I was not stupid, is the key to why I was so successful and continue to be," she told *Forbes* in 2018. "I'm still insecure about it. I don't ever want to be embarrassed again and have someone look at me as a loser, and so I get a lot of ammunition out of that injury."[82]

Corcoran never used her dyslexia as a crutch and instead used it as motivation to become one of the most successful real estate tycoons in New York.

"It made me more creative, more social, and more competitive," she said. "There's a great freedom to being dyslexic . . . *if* you can avoid labeling yourself as a loser in a school system that measures people by As and Bs. And the kids that are so good at school, that don't have to fight for it, very often they don't do as well in life and business because they're not flexible. There's no system dictated to them out there like it is in school and they certainly tend not to make good entrepreneurs."[83]

Kevin O'Leary, aka "Mr. Wonderful," is another one of the stars on *Shark Tank*. Doctors diagnosed O'Leary with dyslexia while he was growing up in Canada after he struggled with both math and reading.

In his memoir, *Cold Hard Truth: On Business, Money & Life*, he describes how his educational therapists restored his confidence.[84] According to *Entrepreneur*, these therapists told young O'Leary, "You have the ability to read backwards, read in a mirror, read upside down. Can any of your classmates do that?"

Ever since, O'Leary, an ultrasuccessful venture capitalist, has called his dyslexia a "superpower." See what "Mr. Wonderful" did? He twisted a negative label into a positive one.

"The way to look at dyslexia is as a unique power instead of an affliction," O'Leary said in 2016. "Very few people have the abilities that dyslexics have. If you look down the road, as they grow, what happens to dyslexic men and women is they become very successful in business. This is because dyslexia gives you some really unique perspectives and abilities that I'd call superpowers."[85]

In fact, studies have suggested that there is a much higher occurrence of dyslexia in entrepreneurs like Barbara and Kevin than in the general population. A study by London's Cass Business School in 2009 suggested that "there is a significantly higher incidence of dyslexia in entrepreneurs" and "some of the strategies they adopt to overcome dyslexia (such as delegation of tasks) may be useful in business."[86]

Charles Schwab, the founder and chairman

of the discount brokerage firm that bears his name, struggled to read and write as a child, and admittedly "bluffed" his way through school. When he reached Stanford University, however, he flunked freshman English and French. Even as an adult, Schwab relied on dictation tools. He never figured out the cause of his learning differences until his eight-year-old son suffered the same problems and was two reading levels behind his classmates.

"I remember some of the most brilliant people at Stanford who were scholars and got incredible awards of recognition," Schwab told *Stanford Magazine* in 1999, "but they had no clue about how to get out of a wet paper bag socially. In my case, I knew I wasn't that smart, in English anyway. But I've always felt that I had very strong conceptual capabilities. I could imagine things much faster than some other people who were stuck thinking sequentially. That helped me in solving complicated business problems. I could visualize how things would look at the end of the tunnel."[87]

As of August 2021, the Charles Schwab Corporation controls $7.6 trillion in client assets.[88] In 1990, Charles Schwab and his wife, Helen, launched the Schwab Foundation for Learning to help families cope with learning differences.

Bullies probably called Anthony Robles a "cripple" more than once. He was born with just one leg. As a kid, he hid his prosthetic leg so his mother wouldn't make him wear it.[89] Anthony found his calling as a wrestler when he was fourteen. Even with only one leg, he became one of the best in wrestlers in the country, winning two high school state championships and going 96–0 as a senior. Still, college coaches had their doubts about his abilities, so just one school, Arizona State University, offered him a scholarship. There, he earned another label that will stay with him forever—national champion.[90] In 2011, he won an NCAA individual title in the 125-pound weight class.[91]

"I always get asked what kept me going through the hard times," Robles told ESPN. "It took me nine years to win a national title. But during the hard times I wrote down my goals. In high school I wrote down 'state champion' on a sticky note. I still have that notepad in my trophy case. In college, I wrote down 'national champion.' I posted it in my locker so I would see it every day when I went to practice. It helped me hold myself accountable. Write down whatever you want to accomplish."[92]

What did each of the aforementioned people have in common? They weren't victims and refused to give in to their differences. When we're faced with challenges or obstacles in life, we build amazing qualities like perseverance, stamina, grit, and self-belief. I firmly believe that if you go through life without

Labels are for jars— not people.

obstacles, you're going to coast and not accomplish anything meaningful. People like Tim Tebow and Charles Schwab didn't believe the superficial labels others tried to place on them.

What I've learned in my life, perhaps more than anything else, is that labels are for jars—not people. Have you ever tried to remove one of those annoying labels off an item you purchased on Amazon or a Christmas gift you unwrapped? As soon as you start peeling it, the label tears apart and leaves half of itself and, worse, sticky glue behind. Most of the time, you can't peel it off with your fingernails or scrub it off with a rag. Even after you soak it in soapy hot water, there's still unsightly residue left behind. It's the worst!

Now imagine how people feel when they have been labeled. They can't peel off what others say about them. The painful words can't be undone or scrubbed away. Instead of using labels to demean people or bring them down, let's choose words that inspire them to reach their fullest potential and encourage them to be authentic and original—to be themselves. If we must use labels, let's choose the good ones like:

- kind
- sweet
- considerate
- thoughtful
- smart
- funny
- optimistic
- bold
- loyal
- loving
- interesting
- beautiful

More than anything else, remember that your words carry weight. As Proverbs 18:21 says: "The tongue has the power of life and death, and those who love it will eat its fruit." We must choose our words carefully and be slow to speak. We have to think about how our words will make others feel.

I still believe labels should be left to jars and clothes. If we must use them, our tongues should choose words that build others up, not ones that tear others down. Think before you speak. Be thoughtful. Be kind.

CHAPTER EIGHT

Stretch Yourself

....

BELIEVE IT OR NOT, there are more than 70 million results available when you Google "uses of a rubber band." Some of the ways you can use them are well known and practical, like rolling up a newspaper or magazine, tying your hair, tie-dyeing a shirt, saving a remote control, and keeping a bread bag closed. Others might not be so familiar, such as keeping sliced apples fresh,[93] removing stripped screws,[94] and turning regular jeans into maternity pants.[95]

Rubber bands come in a variety of shapes, sizes, and colors, and, as you probably know, they're very, very flexible. There are hundreds or even thousands of uses for rubber bands, but rubber bands are only helpful when we stretch them. If you've ever been on the wrong end of a rubber band flung across the room, you know how much energy one can produce—and how much it hurts!

We're the same way—physically, emotionally, and spiritually. We can't reach our full potentials if we don't stretch ourselves and utilize all our energy. At times, God tests us by stretching us to extremes to encourage us to use everything He has provided us. And if I've learned anything in life, it's that God has made me flexible by throwing almost anything and everything at me.

Only a few weeks after the school psychologist told my parents that I was going to be illiterate for life, I faced one of my greatest medical challenges. It was during the fall of 2005, which was my first season playing football for the Grosse Pointe Red Barons.

At times, God tests us by stretching us to extremes to encourage us to use everything He has provided us.

I was small for a ten-year-old, but my coach, Tony Cimmarrusti, played me at center in the middle of the offensive line. I was tough and physical for my size and didn't complain much about the physical nature of the sport because, let's face it, I'd dealt with pain and being uncomfortable for much of my life. Yet, I have to admit, my legs and back often ached after practices and games. I did my best to hide my discomfort from my coaches and parents. It was harder to keep my secret when my neck started twitching like I had Tourette's syndrome. I didn't tell my parents or anyone else because I feared they would make me quit playing.

Finally, during one of our games near the end of the season, I couldn't tolerate the pain any longer. After a series of plays, I hobbled off the field to our bench. I shifted my shoulder pads under my red uniform. Mom and Dad came down from the metal bleachers to check on me. "Hey, J, did you get hurt in the game?" Dad asked me.

"No, I've been hurting for a while, Dad, on and off," I admitted.

Mom had a very concerned look on her face. "Remember, he has a high pain tolerance," she told Dad. "And he doesn't always tell us when he's in pain."

When we got home, Mom called my pediatrician, Dr. Douglas Ziegler. I knew what that meant: more tests and who knows what else. When we arrived at Dr. Ziegler's office the next day, he told me to walk to the nurse's desk and back. I walked up the hallway, trying not to limp. My body tingled and my neck was stiff. I could barely bend over and touch my toes.

Initially, Dr. Ziegler ordered an X-ray and saw nothing wrong. Then he did blood tests, which didn't turn up any red flags. He advised my parents to keep an eye on me and sent me home. Only a few days later, however, Dr. Ziegler called and told Mom that he had woken up in the middle of the night worried about me. He wanted to order an MRI just to make certain there wasn't something serious going on with me.

I had an MRI on January 27, 2006. After Dr. Ziegler and other physicians read my results, I was diagnosed with tethered spinal cord syndrome. Of course, I was too young to know what having a tethered spinal cord meant. As it turned out, my parents were all too familiar with the frightening condition. For whatever reason, there's a high incidence of tethered spinal cord syndrome in people with VATER association, especially if they've had a perforated anus like me.[96] Because I was at greater risk, my parents had monitored me for symptoms over the years, such as weakness in my legs, lower back pain, and scoliosis.

As a child, I'd had severe headaches, which led to many MRIs to make sure my spinal cord wasn't tethered. Each one came back clean. I'd had back pain over the years as well; going to the chiropractor, stretching, and massages usually made it go away.

According to the National Institute of Neurological Disorders and Stroke, tethered spinal cord syndrome is a "neurological disorder caused by tissue attachments that limit the movement of the spinal cord within the spinal column. Attachments may occur congenitally at the base of the spinal cord . . . or they may develop near the site of an injury to the spinal cord. . . . The course of the disorder is progressive."[97]

In other words, it wasn't good and there was

a chance my condition might get much worse. The spinal cord is the long cylinder of nerves that runs from the base of the brain stem through the vertebral canal to the bottom of the spine. It is like a power cord to the entire central nervous systems, carrying incoming and outgoing messages between the brain and the rest of the body. When fibers from the spinal cord become attached to tissue around the spine, the cord can become tethered as it is stretched—and damaged—as the spine grows.

In many ways, a tethered spinal cord is exactly like a tightly stretched rubber band. If you put a rubber band under extreme pressure for an extended period of time, we all know what the outcome will be. It'll snap. Tethered spinal cord syndrome can cause scar tissue to develop, which might inhibit the flow of fluids around the spinal cord. This can cause cysts to form in the spinal cord, which can lead to a loss of movement, chronic pain, trouble walking, and even permanent paralysis.[98] It was serious.

Immediately doctors told me that I had to stop playing sports. No more football. No more lacrosse. It wasn't the news a sports-loving, ten-year-old boy wanted to hear. Remember what I said about being flexible? Once again, life—and the good Lord—gave me lemons, so I made lemonade. I became a manager for the lacrosse team the next spring and learned to appreciate the game that way, cheering for my friends and teammates all season long.

Dr. Ziegler advised my parents to find a pediatric neurosurgeon as quickly as possible. Mom and Dad had a consultation with Dr. Steven Hamm, a neurosurgeon at Children's Hospital of Michigan. Dr. Hamm explained to them how he would complete the delicate surgery by cutting and removing portions of the vertebrae in my back to untether my spinal cord. He also ordered two additional MRIs to make certain I didn't have something called Chiari malformation, a condition in which brain tissue extends into the spinal column. According to the Mayo Clinic, Chiari malformation occurs "when part of your skull is abnormally small or misshapen, pressing on your brain and forcing it downward."[99] Thankfully, the tests confirmed that I didn't have that condition.

Mom and Dad wanted a second opinion, so they called Dr. Alberto Peña, who by then had moved from New York to Cincinnati Children's Hospital. He recommended Dr. Kerry Crone, one of Dr. Peña's fellow surgeons at the hospital. Mom and Dad sent Dr. Crone my medical records and MRI images, and we left for a short trip to my grandparents' winter home in Key Largo, Florida.

During the flight to the Florida Keys, pain shot up and down my lower back and leg. That night, I lost control of my bladder and had an accident in bed, which hadn't happened in a very long time. Mom and

Dad didn't tell me at the time, but the loss of bowel and bladder control is a sign that tethered spinal cord syndrome is becoming more serious.

The next morning, Mom called Dr. Crone's office and described my worsening symptoms to one of his nurses. The nurse promised that someone would get back to us as quickly as possible. Even so, Dad and I, along with both my grandfathers and our friend Shawn, decided to go offshore fishing. By the time Dr. Crone called Mom back, we were five miles offshore—with three sixty- to eighty-pound sailfish set on lines!

After asking Mom a few quick questions about my symptoms, Dr. Crone said, "What you are describing to me is nerve damage. JT's tethered cord is causing him a possibly irreversible situation. He needs surgery ASAP. Where are you?"

Mom told him we were in the Florida Keys.

"Mrs. Mestdagh," Dr. Crone said sternly, "you need to do whatever you can to get to Cincinnati as soon as possible. It's absolutely essential."

After hanging up the phone, Mom sat down and tried to collect her thoughts. She couldn't help but cry. My parents had tried to keep my grandparents generally informed of my health without sharing so many intimate details that they would worry. There was no hiding it this time. My grandmothers consoled Mom, and they agreed that she had to call Dad to get me home.

After taking a few deep breaths, Mom called Dad's cell phone. "Jim, JT has to get to Cincinnati Children's Hospital now. His tethered cord has become very bad."

Dad was screaming over the engine's noise and didn't want to alarm everyone else on the boat. "We have a triple-on right now and it is extremely chaotic at the moment! I'll call you back."

Dad waited until I landed my fish, took a few photographs, then released it back into the crystal-blue water. Then he returned Mom's call and heard the full frightening update. We headed back to shore— and I didn't know exactly why. That night, after a wonderful dinner of fresh grouper and snapper that we'd caught only hours earlier, my parents told me we had to get to Cincinnati for surgery as soon as possible. We were flying back home to Detroit the next morning to unpack and repack our suitcases for cold weather, and then we'd be heading to the hospital in Ohio.

On February 20, 2006, we met with Dr. Crone and another surgeon who were going to perform the procedure. Dr. Crone said my tethered cord was low in my spine and very, very tight. The good news was, he was confident he could release it by going through the vertebrae rather than taking them out. I had more X-rays, blood work, and bladder tests. We finally went back to our hotel and had dinner.

The next morning, while Mom was returning to our hotel room after working out, she ran into Grace Fenton, our family friend who had driven to Cincinnati to see me. As luck would have it, Grace was staying in the same hotel as us. When Mom came back to our room, I told her that I wished I could see a friend. She told me that she'd go try to find me one and that I would owe her five dollars if she did. When Mrs. Fenton arrived at the surgical waiting room that day, I was so happy to see her—even if I was five dollars poorer!

Shortly before my surgery started at 3:00 p.m., Dad's cell phone rang. He answered and then handed me the phone. It was Pa, my paternal grandfather, who was back at his home in Vero Beach, Florida. He told me they were praying for me.

"Don't worry, Pa," I told him. "Jesus will take care of me."

Although I was worried, I believed what I had said. I knew in my heart, even as a ten-year-old, that God was close by and had felt my pain and anxiety, and that He had heard each one of my prayers. I knew He would be right there in the operating room with me, holding my right hand. God would personally be with me, giving me comfort and strength and providing the surgeons with wisdom and steady hands. I remembered Isaiah 43:2:

When you pass through the waters,
I will be with you;
and when you pass through the rivers,
they will not sweep over you.
When you walk through the fire,
you will not be burned;
the flames will not set you ablaze.

I had never passed through waters so high, a river so rough, or flames so intense. I knew I was safe and wouldn't be alone, however, because God was always with me. Mrs. Fenton came into the room, prayed with me, and hugged me. So did Mom and Dad. I took deep breaths so I wouldn't cry. I knew there was a possibility that I could wake up paralyzed and never walk again.

The surgery lasted three hours. Dr. Crone made an incision in my lower back and removed tiny portions of the wings of my L4 and L5 vertebrae in the lumbar region, right above the sacrum. Then he gently opened the dura mater, the thick membrane protecting my spinal cord, and searched for the exact location where my spinal cord was attached. With pure heart, clear head, and a steady hand, he released the cord successfully.

Dr. Crone finally walked out of the operating room around six o'clock. I'm sure the three-hour surgery seemed much longer than that for my parents.

Dr. Crone told Mom and Dad that the procedure had gone exactly as he had hoped. I was awake and could feel my legs and toes. I would be walking better soon, Dr. Crone promised, and my back and neck pain would be gone. Dr. Crone told my parents that when he released my tethered spinal cord, "It literally shot up, like a rubber band!"

My pain was absolutely excruciating for the next few days. Since my back muscles had been cut, my vertebrae split, and my spinal cord released, I wasn't permitted to move. I had to lie flat for days. You might think that would be difficult for a ten-year-old, but I was so uncomfortable that I didn't want to move an inch. I slept much of the time. My parents were in the room with me, but the lights had to be dim. Nurses came in and out of the room to monitor my blood pressure, temperature, and medication levels. Respiratory therapists checked my breathing.

I knew in my heart, even as a ten-year-old, that God was close by and had felt my pain and anxiety, and that He had heard each one of my prayers.

The first night, my temperature spiked to 103.5 degrees. Doctors checked my blood and urine for an infection but didn't find one. A chest X-ray revealed that mucus was building up in my lungs. My blood pressure was also low; doctors believed it was probably caused by the heavy doses of morphine I was receiving.

By the next day, I was showing signs of improvement and acting more like myself. Physical therapy was painful, and I couldn't do much the first couple of days. By Friday, doctors ordered me to get out of bed. It took me forty minutes. Yes, forty minutes! Making my body move even a fraction of an inch was painful. It hurt so much I couldn't help but scream, "My back! My back!"

It would have been rather easy for a ten-year-old boy to give in to the pain. Even back then, however, I was determined to stretch myself and get back on my feet. By Sunday, I had already walked around the hospital floor three times. Later that day, Dr. Crone delivered the good news.

"My patients usually are here for at least ten days, JT," Dr. Crone told me. "But you are doing wonderfully. I am not sure why I am doing this, but I'd like to send you home early because you are doing so well."

I looked at Mom and Dad and couldn't help but grin.

"I know how this happened, Dr. Crone," I said. "I have so many people all over the world praying for me—and God was with me and answered their prayers!"

After recovering at home for several weeks, I spent much of that spring at my grandparents' home in the Keys. The warm weather helped my back, and I was able to swim in their pool with my dog, Duke. I wasn't walking fast or running yet, but I was able to move a lot. Mom and a tutor homeschooled me there, and Dad came down to see us nearly every weekend. Mom and I stayed until May. I was strong enough to go to camp that summer.

* * *

Compared to the first ten years of my life, the next four were pretty uneventful in terms of my health. After the incident with the headmaster of University Liggett School and moving to the Denver Academy, I was homeschooled for much of middle school. Then I went back to University Liggett School for the ninth grade—four years after getting kicked out. There was a new administration, a new philosophy of education, and even a new student support services department. We were hopeful it would work this time.

Obviously, former school administrators had asked me to leave when I was younger, and many kids might not have accepted the challenge of going back to a place where they were previously uninvited. Not me. I looked forward to taking advantage of opportunities the new administration was affording me and being a test pilot for kids with learning differences who might end up there in the future. I wasn't afraid to stretch myself—even if the first few weeks were uncomfortable.

Thanks to people like Dr. Joseph P. Healey, the head of school; Beth Beckmann, the associate head of school and dean of faculty; and Michelle Ondersma, a licensed clinical psychologist, I was able to flourish as a freshman. I asked my teachers for accommodations and became my own biggest advocate. Almost all my teachers were flexible and worked with me to help me learn. Dr. Healey's vision of Curriculum for Understanding, which allowed students to pilot their own academic growth, helped provide me a blueprint for achieving. Dr. Healey was opposed to "sorting" kids based on test scores, numbers, or data. He knew there were kids like me who learned differently.

Things were going well, but once again my body had other ideas. In February 2011, I started experiencing severe back pain. I constantly cracked my neck and back to relieve pain and stiffness and asked my parents for back rubs. I rolled on a foam roller on the floor to help alleviate the pain and even tried an inversion table. Nothing seemed to work.

Things in the plumbing department weren't good either. We weren't sure what was going on. I had appointments scheduled at Cincinnati Children's Hospital the next month. Mom wanted to make sure nothing serious was happening, so I had an MRI at a local hospital. The doctors there gave me an "all clear."

In Cincinnati, I had a scoliosis X-ray and an abdominal X-ray, as well as an urodynamics test that measured how efficiently my bladder emptied. My urologist, Dr. Pramod P. Reddy, whom I had been seeing since I was ten years old, confirmed that my bladder was twice the size of a typical fifteen-year-old's. He still didn't think that was the cause of my current problems, though, so he ordered more tests.

Next, I had an appointment with Dr. Crone, who had done my tethered cord surgery five years earlier. Dr. Crone had seen the MRI from the Detroit hospital, didn't like it, and worried something might be wrong. When technicians take an MRI of your spinal column, they're looking to make sure the spinal cord is floating in the fluid in the column. Since the radiologists in Detroit had taken the MRI while I was lying on my back, which allowed the cord to kind of settle down in the column, Dr. Crone wasn't sure it was an "all clear." He ordered another MRI with me lying on my stomach.

Early the next morning, we returned to Dr. Crone's office. He was unavailable so we met with

Mimi, his nurse. She showed us the scan. Right away, we could see what was wrong. I started to choke up. Mom's eyes watered. Dad swallowed hard.

My spinal cord was tethered again.

We left the office and wandered into the long hallway. I stared out the window at the Cincinnati skyline. I was trying to hold back tears, but my head was about to explode. Finally, I let it out. I'd had more than a dozen surgeries by then, but none had been as painful as the one on my spine. The first time, my body hurt from head to toe. No recovery had been more difficult or lasted so long. I knew this time might be even worse because I was five years older. Once I came to grips with the situation, I leaned my shoulder against the cold window and sobbed. I could hear my parents crying behind me too.

Dad took me into the restroom. I splashed my face with water.

"We're going to take it one day at a time, J" he told me. "We'll get through this."

Retethering the spinal cord occurs in as many as 25 percent of patients with tethered spinal cord syndrome, according to neuroscientists from the University of California, San Diego.[100] It's rare, and I was on the wrong side of the statistics. Surgery for a retethered cord can be more difficult because of scar tissue and adhesions to the spinal cord, dura mater, and spinal nerve roots. Once again, I faced the terrifying possibility of not being able to walk.

About a month later, I returned to Cincinnati Children's Hospital for the surgery. When Dr. Crone opened my spinal column for the second time, he couldn't believe what he saw. I had two spots of tethering—one at the original spot and another slightly below it. He had never seen that before. Once again, God was with me, and I could feel His presence. The surgery was a success.

When I woke up, I was suffering from severe back spasms. The pain medication made me sick, and I was throwing up left and right. Two days after the surgery, Dad ordered me out of bed to walk. The recovery was as bad as I feared it would be. But eventually, I was able to go home and begin my rehabilitation.

Since my recovery would last a while, the administrators at University Liggett School agreed to let my final grades be what they were when I left for the hospital. I made up a few assignments and tests that summer, but overall my freshman year was a success.

On June 13, 2011, I returned to school for an end-of-the-year awards celebration. I sat in my chair and clapped for my classmates. Given my academic situation, I had no expectation of hearing my name called.

One of the final awards was the TiJuan Kidd Prize, which is named after a sophomore who tragically died in the summer of 1987. When Dr. Healey called my name to accept the award, I was completely surprised. My parents had surprised looks and wide smiles on their faces too. I walked to the stage, and I still remember my classmates clapping for me. Everything I had endured that year—the pain, anxiety, fear, and worry of the unknown—was gone.

Obviously, I didn't know TiJuan Kidd; he had attended University Liggett School nearly a quarter-century before me. But his story of perseverance, conviction, and honor is one that continues to inspire me.

TiJuan Kidd was born to a seventeen-year-old single mother on June 23, 1972. According to the *Detroit Free Press,* he was born premature and weighed only three pounds, three ounces. When his weight dropped to two pounds, doctors feared he might not make it. His grandmother urged her young daughter to give him up for adoption. At the hospital, his mother, Rhonda Kidd-Love, held him in her arms and whispered, "I don't know how we're going to make it, but we're sure going to try. It'll just be you and I against the world."[101]

TiJuan didn't know his biological father until he was a teenager. His uncle murdered his aunt when he was seven. When he was fourteen, one of his friends was killed and stuffed in a dumpster. The *Detroit Free Press* wrote this about him in November 1987: "He had known death all his life. He had feared it, respected it and defied it with the easy grin and steady good humor for which he came to be admired both at home in Detroit and in his other world—the rarefied atmosphere of the prestigious University Liggett School in Grosse Pointe Woods."[102]

With his determined mother's help and encouragement, TiJuan blossomed into a good student and an exceptional athlete. He was awarded a scholarship to University Liggett School, where he played on the basketball team and was preparing to become the starting quarterback on the football team. He and a friend from his neighborhood in Detroit took a seventeen-mile bus ride to and from school. By the end of his freshman year at University Liggett School, he was very popular among his classmates and teachers.

On July 18, 1987, TiJuan attended a friend's birthday party in Detroit. While dancing in the friend's basement, TiJuan and others heard that a group of boys were going to crash the party. He went outside with a couple of friends to assess the situation. A block or so from the house, they noticed people hiding in bushes. TiJuan and his friends turned and ran. A seventeen-year-old boy shot TiJuan in the back of the head and killed him. He was fifteen years old. No one was ever convicted of his murder.

At a memorial for TiJuan at University Liggett School shortly after his death, one student talked about how TiJuan had reached out to him when he was sitting alone in the lunchroom. "He rose my spirits quite a bit.

When you stretch yourself and reach for the seemingly impossible, God steps in and makes the unimaginable possible.

It meant a lot, how nice he was to me." Others talked about TiJuan's wide smile, warm demeanor, good manners, and his ability to blend in with practically anyone.[103]

Though his life was unfairly cut short, TiJuan used the fifteen years he had here on this earth to stretch himself and reach his potential. How far have you stretched yourself? Are you reaching your full potential like TiJuan? Or are you only settling for mediocrity and the status quo? Stretching yourself requires a change, and that's uncomfortable for many. Believe me, I know. However, when you stretch yourself and reach for the seemingly impossible, God steps in and makes the unimaginable possible. God knows your full potential, and He doesn't want you settling for anything less. Stretch yourself. Take chances. Be versatile like a rubber band. And remember to be kind to others like TiJuan. That's the greatest legacy you can leave.

CHAPTER NINE

Listen to Others

....

HOW MANY TIMES in our lives have we thought to ourselves, *If I had only listened?* If only we had stopped and listened, we might have been able to help a friend in need. If only we had stopped and listened to instructions, we might have completed a task right the first time instead of having to do it again. If only we had stopped and listened to Mom, we would have avoided stepping in the dog poop in the yard.

When you listen to others, you learn about someone else. In the process, you'll probably learn something about yourself too. The sweetest sound to a person is the sound of their name. When you say someone else's name, it means you were truly listening. Remember, there's a reason God gave us two ears and only one mouth. He wants us to listen to others—and Him. Before we understand others, we need to know their past experiences. We need to listen to their stories to truly understand them. As the old saying goes, we need to walk in their shoes. We need to walk beside them until our shoes begin to feel like theirs.

I'm certain of one thing: I'm glad others listened

Remember, there's a reason God gave us two ears and only one mouth. He wants us to listen to others —and Him.

to me—and walked in my shoes—in my greatest times of need, and I'm thankful that God listened to my prayers.

During my junior year at University Liggett School in 2013, I began to seriously think about where I would attend college, which at one time had seemed impossible for me. Since I was doing well in school and my grades were good, I independently decided that I wouldn't limit myself. I was going to apply to a handful of Ivy League schools, including Princeton University, and wasn't going to sell myself short.

The director of college guidance, on the other hand, had ideas of her own. When we had a meeting to discuss my potential college choices, her list didn't include Ivy League institutions. When I asked her why, she said, "Why waste your time, JT?"

Others were far more supportive, including another counselor, Beth Beckmann. She told me about one of her former students, a young man named Forrest. There was a photograph of him on her desk.

When I asked about Forrest, she said, "At my school in New York, we took in a seventh grader who also had learning issues. I kind of shepherded him through. He ended up at Princeton." I went home and told my parents that I wanted to be the "Forrest of Liggett."

I knew being accepted into a college that interested me was going to be an uphill climb. Not every school out there has programs for students with learning differences and having access to those resources was at the top of my list of priorities. Yet in my heart, I knew I'd worked too hard to lower my expectations. With help and dedication from a lot of kind people, I'd put myself in a position to graduate from high school with a high GPA.

I also continued to work with Steve Tattum whenever he was in Michigan, which was typically four times a year, and I joined him when he trained teachers in the state to share my improvements and experiences in the F.A.S.T. Reading System.

Over time, I became my own advocate. I asked teachers for help when I needed it and fought for accommodations when I thought they were necessary.

In the summer of 2013, my parents and I flew to North Carolina to visit a trio of colleges that we had identified as strong possibilities: Elon University, Guilford College, and High Point University. I was also considering Curry College in Milton, Massachusetts, which was the first university in the country to provide academically focused assistance to college-able students with learning differences.

We knew very little about High Point—a liberal arts college that was founded in 1924 and is affiliated with the United Methodist Church.[104] It is located in the Piedmont Triad region of North Carolina, about ninety miles west of Raleigh. We didn't have any family or friends who had attended High Point, and no one from University Liggett had ever gone to school there, so my teachers and counselors were unfamiliar with it as well.

The day before my official college tours, Dad thought it would be a good idea to drive to each of the campuses to get to know our way around. High Point was our last stop that day, and a purple LED sign in a parking space for special guests greeted us when we arrived. It read:

JT Mestdagh
University Liggett
Grosse Pointe, MI

We climbed out of our rental car and strolled around campus. High Point was a beautifully mani-cured campus with massive neoclassical brick build-ings. I could hear faint classical music coming from somewhere. I'm not kidding. I felt like Kevin Costner in *Field of Dreams*.

Is this heaven? No, it's North Carolina, I thought to myself.

Immediately, I knew High Point was a place where I could spend the next four years. Dad suggested we find the Earl N. Phillips School of Business since I was interested in majoring in a subject related to that field. We located the stately two-story structure with four giant white columns. We stepped inside, where everything was new and elegant.

We returned to the promenade, a wide central greenway lined with international flags. I'm telling you, everything about the campus was perfect. I was more than certain that I wanted to be a student at High Point after only a few minutes on campus. "I'm going here," I whispered to myself.

Just then, the doors to Hayworth Chapel swung open, and students with wide smiles started making their way down the steps. High Point holds chapel service every Wednesday at 5:30 p.m., and the service was just ending. As we watched the students pour out, a distinguished-looking man walked among the students, smiling and chatting. Dad recognized him. It was Dr. Nido R. Qubein, the president of High Point University.

President Qubein noticed us, and even though we were a family he knew nothing about, he walked over and introduced himself. President Qubein had been a very successful entrepreneur, businessman, and consultant before moving to higher education. More than anything else, he is a master of personal communication. He has written books about communicating effectively, given thousands of motivational speeches, and consulted with many Fortune 500 companies.[105] After only a few minutes, it was easy to understand why. He asked about my aspirations and goals and even complimented the red driving shoes that I was wearing. He listened intently and made me feel like no one else was on campus in that moment, like all great leaders do.

President Qubein gave us a brief tour of campus and suggested that we have dinner at one of the campus restaurants. Then his cell phone rang. It was his wife, who asked where he was. His family had been waiting on him to come home to celebrate one of his son's birthdays. Before heading home, President Qubein drove us to the 1924 Prime chophouse.

When I told Mom and Dad that I wanted to go to school there, Mom's heart sank. She worried that the odds of High Point accepting me were stacked against me, and she didn't want me to be disappointed. But deep down, I knew that's where I was supposed to go. It was just a feeling that I had, like a tap on the shoulder from the Holy Spirit.

Three weeks later, my acceptance letter arrived from High Point University. It was one of the happiest days of my life. President Qubein could appreciate the health problems, learning differences, and other obstacles I had overcome throughout my life. He is a brilliant man in good health, yet he himself overcame so much as a child. After High Point accepted me, Dad sent President Qubein his own pair of the red driving shoes I had been wearing on campus. Then he could truly walk in my shoes.

President Nido Qubein, who was born in Lebanon, lost his father at age six. His mother, Victoria, was left to care for her three sons and two daughters alone. She had only a fourth-grade education but was blessed with a wealth of knowledge and worked very hard to support her family.[106]

When President Qubein was young, his mother told him, "If you want to be a great person, you must first walk side by side and hand in hand with great people."[107] He took his mother's advice to heart and surrounded himself with great people who would help him excel. When President Qubein was seventeen years old, his mother encouraged him to come to the United States to study. He arrived here with fifty dollars in his pocket and a very limited knowledge of English.[108] He taught himself to speak our native language by learning five new words every day.

Shortly after moving to North Carolina, President Qubein persuaded administrators at Mount Olive College to accept him as an international student. He excelled in his classes, while working for the school and at YMCA summer camps.[109] One of the turning points in President Qubein's life occurred during his sophomore year at Mount Olive. He had saved $375 to purchase an automobile, but the cheapest one he could find cost $750. President Qubein told his housemother, Verta Lawhon, about his dilemma. A retired teacher, Mrs. Lawhon earned about $100 in Social Security benefits and $100 in salary from the college every month. She wasn't a wealthy woman by any stretch of the imagination.

At the end of the month, President Qubein checked his bank account balance and was stunned to find $750. At first, he believed the bank had made an error, but then it hit him: Mrs. Lawhon had doubled his balance by dipping into whatever savings she had. She had listened to his needs and decided to make a real difference in his life. According to his book, *Life Balance the Sufi Way*, Mrs. Lawhon told him, "I've decided it's much better for me to invest my money into the life of a budding young man than to park it in my saving account." That remarkable gesture of kindness left an indelible impression on President Qubein and provided him with a lesson he would never forget: it is better to give than to receive.[110]

During President Qubein's second summer working at the YMCA camp, one of the administrators told him that if he transferred to what was then

High Point College, he could get a job working for the YMCA office.[111]

Shortly before President Qubein left Mount Olive, the university president told him that even though he had been working ten hours a day, his wages hadn't been enough to pay what he owed in tuition, room, and board. In fact, there was a sizable balance. Fortunately, a doctor in a neighboring town had already paid the balance. President Qubein was so moved by the doctor's kind gesture that he wanted to meet him and personally thank him. The doctor wanted to remain anonymous, and President Qubein has never known his identity to this day.

"Nido went to his dormitory room, knelt beside his bed, and made a commitment to God that when he began to earn money, he, too, in some way, would initiate a fund to help students go to college," the authors of *Life Balance the Sufi Way* wrote.[112] Sufism is an ancient teaching of Islam, a belief that "the way to God is via emotions and spirituality rather than through reason," and it celebrates "the intimate relationship of the seeker with Allah."[113]

President Qubein earned his associate's degree in business from Mount Olive College, a bachelor's degree in human relations from High Point University in 1970, and a master of science in business education from the University of North Carolina-Greensboro.[114] All these years later, President

Qubein knows his academic career would have never happened without the kindness of Mrs. Lawhon, whose gift of a car helped him work to earn money for college, and the anonymous doctor. If they hadn't listened to the story of the international student who had worked tirelessly to achieve the American dream, he might have never been able to finish school.

When President Qubein left graduate school, he had $500 in the bank and launched a company that supplied leadership materials for adults working with children at schools, churches, and summer camps. Before too long, he had more than six thousand customers in thirty countries. He became a highly sought motivational speaker and a successful business consultant. Then President Qubein and a few friends started American Bank & Trust,[115] and he has served on the board of directors of BB&T Corporation since 1990,[116] as well as the boards of other corporations and nonprofits.

President Qubein followed through on his promise to God. By 2007, he had given more than 500 scholarships worth $3 million—and many, many more since.[117]

The story of President Qubein and the local doctor reminds me of the heartwarming tale of actor Chadwick Boseman, who died at the age of forty-three in August 2020 after a private four-year battle with colon cancer.[118] When Boseman was a budding drama student at Howard University in Washington, DC, a summer acting program at the British Academy of Dramatic Acting in Oxford invited him to attend. The only problem: Boseman didn't have the money to pay the tuition or the costs of travel to England. Phylicia Rashad, an actress who played Clair Huxtable on the sitcom *The Cosby Show*, approached Denzel Washington to help her pay for Boseman and eight other students to attend the program. Like Mrs. Lawhon from President Qubein's story, Rashad and Washington were attuned to the needs of these young people and decided to make a difference.

"If you want to be a great person, you must first walk side by side and hand in hand with great people."

—PRESIDENT QUBEIN

Boseman never forgot the kind gesture. At the American Film Institute Lifetime Achievement Award ceremony in 2019, Boseman delivered a memorable salute to Washington.

"As fate would have it, I was one of the students

that he paid for," Boseman said in his speech. "Imagine receiving the letter that your tuition for that summer was paid for and that your benefactor was none other than the dopest actor on the planet."[119]

Of course, Boseman went on to become one of the most beloved actors of his generation. He played baseball pioneer Jackie Robinson in *42*, singer James Brown in *Get on Up*, future Supreme Court Justice Thurgood Marshall in *Marshall*, and most famously the first Black Marvel superhero in *Black Panther*.

"There is no 'Black Panther' without Denzel Washington," Boseman said in his AFI speech. "And not just because of me, but my whole cast. That generation stands on your shoulders. The daily battles won, the thousand territories gained, the many sacrifices you made for the culture on film sets through your career, the things you refused to compromise along the way, laid the blueprints for us to follow."[120]

Another one of my favorite stories of paying it forward involves former NFL running back Warrick Dunn. When Dunn was in high school in Baton Rouge, Louisiana, his mother, Betty Smothers, was murdered on January 7, 1993, while escorting a grocery store manager to a bank to make a night deposit. She was thirty-six years old.[121]

Just two days after his eighteenth birthday, Dunn was suddenly the man of the house and was left to care for his five siblings.[122] The community rallied around Dunn and his family so he could fulfill his dream of playing football at Florida State University. He used his mother's life insurance to buy a home for his brothers and sisters, and his grandmother helped care for them while he was at college.[123]

Playing for legendary Seminoles coach Bobby Bowden, Dunn was a three-time All-Atlantic Coast Conference selection and the first FSU running back to achieve three one-thousand-yard rushing seasons.[124] He left as the school's all-time leading rusher and helped the Seminoles win their first national championship in 1993.[125] A first-round pick of the Tampa Bay Buccaneers in the 1997 NFL draft, Dunn was named Rookie of the Year and played twelve seasons of professional football. When he retired, he ranked fourteenth in NFL all-purpose yards history with 15,306 and nineteenth in rushing yards with 10,967.[126]

Dunn was an even better man off the field. According to his charity's website, as a rookie with the Buccaneers, "Warrick founded our Homes for the Holidays program to fulfill his mother's dream of home ownership for single parent families." While partnering with local organizations like Habitat for Humanity, Homes for the Holidays furnishes houses with furniture and other necessities and provides assistance for down payments.[127] By 2021, Dunn's organization had served 194 families in fifteen states.[128] What a remarkable legacy and tribute to his mother.

What do great men like President Qubein, Chadwick Boseman, and Warrick Dunn have in common? Someone listened to their stories, understood their needs, hopes, and desires, and graciously decided to help. The loving housemother and anonymous doctor listened to President Qubein's story and realized how much they could impact his life. Denzel Washington heard Boseman's needs and acted. The city of Baton Rouge and Florida State University provided Dunn aid when he needed it most, and he later paid it forward by helping hundreds of single mothers and their children.

Always listen intently to others and ask them how they feel. Listen to their stories. You might be surprised by their answers. If you don't listen to others, you won't know how you can help and inspire them, which is the greatest gift we can give. Choose your words carefully and take time to listen. The sincerest form of respect is taking the time to truly listen to someone.

With all the modern technology that we have for communicating with one another even across the world, it seems that most people have forgotten how to communicate clearly with those standing right next to them. In particular, listening has become a lost art. That's too bad because knowing how to listen effectively can bring you a lot of benefits. It can strengthen both personal and professional relationships. It can help your marriage and boost your career. Give people your undivided attention, look them in the eyes, and truly listen to what they're telling you.

The sincerest form of respect is taking the time to truly listen to someone.

Remember, as Carl W. Buehner said, others won't always be able to recall everything you say in a conversation, but they'll likely remember how you made them feel.[129] You can uplift those around you, avoid misunderstandings, and strengthen your relationships by practicing these easy listening techniques each day. Your partner, friends, boss, and clients will be impressed. Reap the benefits of knowing the lost art of listening!

Stop and listen. It's the kind thing to do. If you don't listen to others, you won't know how you can help and inspire them. You won't know how many lives you can change and help bring them joy unless you listen.

CHAPTER TEN

Socially Distant

DESPITE MY HEALTH problems and learning differences, I was very fortunate not to be a target of bullying growing up. I think it was probably because I had such a great group of friends who always had my back and because we lived in a town where people genuinely cared about one another.

In fact, I can only recall one incident of being bullied at school, and some sage advice from my father didn't exactly make the situation better. I was attending kindergarten at Grosse Pointe Academy. My cousin Anton was also at the school, and we played together almost every day on the playground at recess.

One day, a couple of guys decided they were going to pick on us. I went home and told Mom and Dad what had happened.

"If it happens again, tell your teacher about it," Dad told me.

Sure enough, a couple of days later, the bullies picked on us again. This time, Dad had different advice for me. I was taking taekwondo classes at the time, so Dad advised me to stand up for myself. As I told you earlier, even though I didn't really enjoy martial arts classes because I couldn't remember the rituals, the sport did instill self-confidence in me and helped me get physically stronger through exercise.

"JT, if they pick on you again, you have to defend yourself," he said. "You have the ability to punch and kick, so if they pick on you again, give them a swift kick to the chest to tell them to back off."

The very next day, when the kid tried to pull me down from the steps leading up to the slide, I kicked him in the chest. When the boy pulled me to the ground, he picked me up by my winter coat. The zipper left a burn down my neck.

When Dad saw the injury that night, he asked me what had happened. I told him about the kid picking me up off the ground.

"What do you mean he picked you up off the ground?" Dad asked me. "How big is this kindergartner?"

"Dad, he's not in kindergarten," I explained. "He's a fifth grader."

Like I said, I was fortunate that other kids didn't bully me. I can't imagine what it's like being a teenager today with so many kids having access to social media and cell phones, which are essentially tools for teenagers to anonymously leave hateful messages or salacious gossip.

A 2019 Cyberbullying Research Center survey of nearly five thousand middle and high school students found that 36.5 percent of respondents reported being cyberbullied.[130] The kids reported being targeted with mean or hurtful comments, online rumors, physical threats, and harmful photos.

Over the last couple of years, I've become pretty active on social media, including Instagram, YouTube, Twitter, and Facebook. As a budding author and motivational speaker, social media provides me with tremendous opportunities to reach a large audience. It's also a great way to keep up with my friends from high school and college, my relatives, and other people I want to stay in touch with. If you're following reputable media outlets, social media is also a great way to monitor the news and sports scores. In so many ways, it makes the world seem just a little bit smaller for all of us.

Other than that, let's be honest: social media can be the absolute gutter of humanity. Twitter makes it too easy for people to hide behind fake handles and avatars and bully others about their looks, political beliefs, relationship statuses, or just about anything else. Facebook is a great place to see photos of your friend's newborn baby or your neighbors' spring break vacation, but sometimes it feels like a place where people are airing too much of their dirty laundry.

Social media has become our country's new addiction. Today, around seven in ten Americans use social media to connect with others according to the Pew Research Center.[131]

Pew's 2021 data also revealed that about 81 percent of Americans watch videos on YouTube, 69 percent use Facebook, 40 percent post on Instagram, 31 percent are on Pinterest, and 23 percent are Twitter users.[132] By 2025, nearly 4.5 billion people are expected to be on social media.[133] The numbers are absolutely staggering.

Take a minute to think about everything else we could be doing if we just set down our cellphones, laptops, and tablets. How much more productive would we be? How much more would we talk to one another face-to-face instead of doing it through direct messages, tweets, and text messages? When was the last time you walked next door or across the street and had a face-to-face conversation with your neighbor over a cup of coffee? In so many ways, we were socially distancing from one another long before the coronavirus pandemic occurred.

Many of us have to use social media for work reasons, and if we have to be on Facebook, Twitter, Instagram, or Pinterest, it's up to each and every one of us to attempt to make those platforms a better community. Just as you should help an elderly neighbor or someone else in need, try to bring kindness to social media as well. You probably don't realize how much power you have to change someone's day with only your fingertips.

If we work together, we can transform social

media into a friendlier place. Commit to doing at least one random act of kindness on social media each day. Reach out to an old friend. Comment politely on someone's photo. Engage in meaningful dialogue with someone, even if their opinion might be different than your own, instead of screaming and yelling at each other like everyone else seemingly does nowadays. Make someone smile. Or better yet, make them laugh very, very hard. Try to be *nice*.

Let's be honest: social media can be the absolute gutter of humanity.

Of course, bullying was a problem long before social media became so popular. You wouldn't believe the celebrities who say they were bullied as kids. Supermodel Cindy Crawford was ridiculed for the mole on her face—which is the very thing that made her so famous and original.[134] Olympic gold medalist Michael Phelps said other kids teased him about the size of his ears, so much so that he wore a baseball hat to try to hide them.[135] Actress Jessica Alba said she was bullied because she's multiethnic and her family didn't have much money.[136] Kids said actress Blake Lively looked like Big Bird when she was young because she was tall and had yellow hair.[137] Singer Justin Timberlake said he was teased simply because he liked to act and sing.[138]

Taylor Swift probably offered the best advice about cyberbullying in an Instagram post to one of her fans who was being bullied:

> This isn't a high school thing or an age thing. It's a people thing. A life thing. It doesn't stop. It doesn't end or change. People cut other people down for entertainment, amusement, out of jealousy, because of something broken inside them. Or for no reason at all.
>
> It's just what they do, and you're a target because you live your life loudly and boldly. You're bright and joyful and so many people are cynical. . . . Just don't let them change you or stop you from singing or dancing around to your favorite song.[139]

Fortunately, celebrities like Swift, Alba, and Lively have told their stories about being bullied to help so many people around the world. We need to hear more stories like theirs because cyberbullying has made bullying so much worse.

But there are also people out there trying to make the cyberworld a happier, warmer, and more positive place. Carlo Acutis was a typical teenager who lived in Milan, Italy. He liked playing *Pokémon* and *Mario Kart*, wearing Nikes and jeans, playing and watching soccer, and talking on his cell phone. At the age of nine, he taught himself how to code on a computer by reading textbooks and soon thereafter was building websites and graphic designs.[140]

"He learned on his own how to animate 3D cartoons on a computer. He never even took a course on how to use Photoshop," his mother, Antonia Salzano, said in an interview. "He would sit on his bed, download instructions on the internet and he was able to understand all these computer programs."[141]

Carlo also was dedicated to his Catholic faith, which inspired his mother to return to the church. She told the *New York Times* that he attended daily Mass from the time he was seven, never missing a day.[142] He ran websites for churches and other religious organizations in Milan.

Even after Carlo was diagnosed with leukemia as a teenager, he built a

Make someone smile. Or better yet, make them laugh very, very hard.

website that cataloged purported miracles from around the world.[143] He also performed nice gestures of his own, buying meals and blankets for the homeless and refugees on the streets near his home.[144] He brought them hot drinks when it was cold. He volunteered at a soup kitchen and helped elderly and disabled neighbors.[145] In so many ways, Carlo did everything he could to be kind to others.

Sadly, Carlo died of leukemia in 2006. He was only fifteen. His good work, both for the church and his community, didn't go unnoticed. His website that documented purported miracles became quite popular among believers. His followers called him the patron saint of the internet.[146]

Pope Francis, in *Christus Vivit*, an apostolic exhortation that he addressed to "young people and to the entire people of God," even referenced Carlo's good works while calling on Christian young people to live life to the fullest with Christ. After discussing the dangers of the digital world, including "loneliness, manipulation, exploitation and violence," pornography, and gambling, Pope Francis offered young people a way out of the madness:

> I remind you of the good news we received as a gift on the morning of the resurrection: that in all the dark or painful situations that we mentioned, there is a way out. For example,

it is true that the digital world can expose you to the risk of self-absorption, isolation and empty pleasure. But don't forget that there are young people even there who show creativity and even genius. That was the case with the Venerable Carlo Acutis.

Carlo was well aware that the whole apparatus of communications, advertising and social networking can be used to lull us, to make us addicted to consumerism and buying the latest thing on the market, obsessed with our free time, caught up in negativity. Yet he knew how to use the new communications technology to transmit the Gospel, to communicate values and beauty.

Carlo didn't fall into the trap. He saw that many young people, wanting to be different, really end up being like everyone else, running after whatever the powerful set before them with the mechanisms of consumerism and distraction. In this way they do not bring forth the gifts the Lord has given them; they do not offer the world those unique personal talents that God has given to each of them. As a result, Carlo said, "everyone is born as an original, but many people end up dying as photocopies." Don't let that happen to you![147]

In his short life, Carlo was truly original and authentic—and was someone we should all try to emulate. While many young people are walking away from the church nowadays, he embraced his beliefs and was inquisitive about his faith, which motivated him to catalog the miracles of Christ and use the internet to spread the gospel across the globe.

"Carlo was the light answer to the dark side of the web," his mother told the *New York Times*. She added that his life "can be used to show how the internet can be used for good, to spread good things."[148]

Following Carlo's tragic death, the Diocese of Assisi in Italy opened an investigation of his life to determine if he lived with sufficient holiness and virtue to be considered for sainthood. The diocese pored over his emails, internet searches,[149] and letters, and interviewed people who knew him to determine if he was truly a "servant of God."[150]

Armed with the evidence, the diocese petitioned the Vatican to consider Carlo for sainthood. The Congregations of the Causes of the Saints examined the evidence and passed it to Pope Francis, who decreed that Carlo had indeed lived a life of "heroic virtue," and thus could be called "venerable."

There is another step to becoming a saint: proof that a miracle has been granted by God through the intercession of the venerable servant of God. In Carlo's case, the miracle occurred through a Brazilian boy named Mattheus who was suffering from a rare pancreatic disorder. The young boy had long struggled to eat and gain weight. In 2013, at four years old, he weighed only twenty pounds, according to the Catholic News Agency, and survived almost solely on protein shakes and vitamins. He was not expected to live much longer.[151]

That same year, which was seven years after Carlo's death, a priest in Mattheus's town obtained a relic from Carlo's mother and then told everyone in his parish to come to Mass and pray for Carlo's intercession of healing. Mattheus and his mother attended the prayer service. Miraculously, Mattheus felt better on the way home. Father Nicola Gori, postulator of the beatification and canonization of Carlo, told Italian media: "On October 12, 2013, seven years after Carlo's death, a child, affected by a congenital malformation (annular pancreas), when it was his turn to touch the picture of the future blessed, expressed a singular wish, like a prayer: 'I wish I could stop vomiting so much.' Healing began immediately, to the point that the physiology of the organ in question changed."[152]

That day, Mattheus went home and ate a meal of steak, french fries, rice, and beans. He didn't vomit. He continued to eat full meals and gained weight. Mattheus's mother told Brazilian media: "Before, I didn't even use my cell phone, I was averse to technology. Carlo changed my way of thinking, he was known for talking about Jesus on the Internet, and I realized that my testimony would be a way to evangelize and give hope to other families."[153]

On October 10, 2020, Carlo was beatified, "or declared 'blessed' by the pope," reported the *New York Times*, which was the next step in him becoming the first millennial saint—though not the first young saint. Of the more than ten thousand saints recognized by the Roman Catholic Church, "120 died as children or teenagers." One of them was nineteen-year-old Joan of Arc.[154]

I guess we can only hope that five hundred years from now people will remember Carlo as much as they do Joan of Arc, who was burned at the stake for dressing as a man and fighting for the French in the Hundred Years' War in the fifteenth century.[155] If Carlo's memory can help persuade people to use social media in a good way, his life might have very well been just as impactful as hers.

Like Carlo, former NBA player Rex Chapman is truly a social media original, even if he was reluctant to become one. Chapman had to have a social media presence in his job as a TV analyst for the University of Kentucky men's basketball and NBA TV. There was only one problem: Chapman hated being on Twitter.

"Yeah, I wanted off of it," Chapman told ESPN in 2020. "I was so tired of it. . . . It's just toxic right now, the political climate. Everything is so snarky."[156]

Chapman, who is now in his fifties, is a basketball legend in Kentucky. He was named the state's Mr. Basketball as a senior at Apollo High School in Owensboro and was named a McDonald's All-American player.[157] He chose to play collegiately at Kentucky, where he was named Southeastern Conference Freshman of the Year and All-SEC in his two seasons there. He was known simply as "King Rex" by Wildcats fans.[158]

In 1988, Chapman was the first player ever drafted by the Charlotte Hornets, with the eighth pick in the first round of the NBA draft.[159] He averaged 16.9 points as a rookie and twice competed in the Slam Dunk Contest at the NBA All-Star game. He spent twelve seasons in the NBA, playing for the Hornets, Washington Bullets, Miami Heat, and Phoenix Suns, averaging 14.6 points per game in his career.[160]

Injuries forced Chapman into retirement, and after an emergency appendectomy, he became addicted to OxyContin. He went to rehab and hit rock bottom when he was arrested for shoplifting merchandise from an Apple store in Scottsdale, Arizona. He intended to sell the goods to pay off gambling debts.[161]

Chapman returned to Kentucky and entered a rehab facility that one of his former teammates operated. He got clean and went back to work.

Chapman's time in the social media spotlight began when he decided he would do something different from what everyone else was doing on Twitter. He became an original. He posted a funny video of a dolphin knocking an unsuspecting person off his paddleboard. He included the cutline: "Block or charge?" a reference to one of the more controversial officiating decisions in basketball, and it wasn't lost on most of the people who saw it. Including retweets and shares, the video has been viewed more than 10 million times.[162]

Today Chapman has over a million Twitter followers who are rewarded with adorable videos of puppies and dogs, a groom surprising his bride by having her students with Down syndrome serve as ring bearers at their wedding,[163] and a mother who built a contraption so her son with cerebral palsy could skateboard for the first time.[164] As Chapman likes to say, "This is the Twitter content I'm here for."[165]

Chapman looks for the good stuff on the internet and shares it with the world.

"I just think that everybody likes good things," Chapman told ESPN. "Everybody likes dogs, everybody likes to feel good and believe the best in people. I think right now, if it's providing anything, it's just a little laugh during the day, just to remind yourself that we all just have thoughts in our heads out there. We think, we write, and we're all people just trying to get along out there. So let's laugh a little bit."[166]

Amen. Chapman isn't the only celebrity trying to make social media a kinder, gentler place for everyone. Canadian singer-songwriter Shawn Mendes often reminds his fans on social media to be kind to others. He has even been seen wearing a yellow T-shirt that reads, "TREAT PEOPLE WITH KINDNESS."

Mendes, who was born in 1998, learned how to play the guitar by watching YouTube videos.[167] He started posting six-second videos of himself singing cover songs on Vine, which led to his first record deal in 2014.[168] It also caused older boys to bully him at school.

"[They were] yelling out 'sing for me Shawn sing for me!' In a way that made me feel absolutely horrible . . . like what I was doing was just stupid & wrong," Mendes wrote in a June 2019 Instagram post.

"It's not a joke to me. . . . Every single person deserves to do what makes them feel alive. . . . You deserve to follow your heart."[169]

In 2017, Mendes became the first artist to have three number one singles on the *Billboard* Adult Contemporary chart before age twenty,[170] and in 2018 he beat his own record when he landed a fourth single at number one just before his twentieth birthday.[171] He has released four albums;[172] toured North and South America, Europe, Asia, and Australia; and has been nominated for a GRAMMY

Social media would be such a better place if we avoided judging and intimidating others.

three times. More than anything else, though, Mendes wants to be kind.

"I'm trying to be nice all the time," Mendes said in a 2017 interview with CBC. "I think it's important. I really believe in karma. I try to just do things that I want to happen back to me. . . . I think it's important for everybody to just be kind to everyone."[173]

Mendes is also backing up his words with action. During the COVID-19 pandemic, he sent two hundred Cuban sandwiches to frontline workers at Miami's Jackson South Medical Center. A week earlier, they surprised patients at Children's National Hospital in Washington, DC, with a virtual chat.[174]

Isn't being kind on social media so much better than making snarky or mean comments to someone you probably don't even know? Isn't it so much better to help some rise up to their full potential and happiness instead of tearing them down with criticism? Social media would be such a better place if we avoided judging and intimidating others. Truly think about what you're going to write before you send.

If you have to use social media, remember to be like Carlo. Be an original. If you have to be a photocopy, make sure it's of him. Even better, put down your phone, close your laptop, and have real, face-to-face conversations with others. Look them in the eyes. Hear their voices. Be kind. Be true to yourself.

CHAPTER ELEVEN

Learn to Fall

AS SOON AS I could walk, my dad put me in a pair of skis and towed me around the bunny slopes at Beaver Creek Resort in Colorado. My grandparents had built a ski-in ski-out home there in its early development, and my parents started taking me there for holidays when I was just three months old. It became my second home.

It was by God's purpose, not chance, that I met Ladislav Lettovsky there during the Christmas holidays in 2003. At just eight years old, I had absolutely no idea how to pronounce his name. Fortunately, his nickname, "Ladi," was much easier for me to remember.

When I met Ladi, my skiing skills were pretty basic. I was easily cruising down the blue trails and could get from point A to point B on more challenging runs. But I still had a long way to go as far as becoming an advanced skier.

I had worked the previous few seasons with a different instructor. When that instructor informed my parents that he had a scheduling conflict, they figured he was tired of working with a kid who had bathroom challenges. They couldn't blame him.

From the moment I met Ladi I liked him immensely. Yet I have to admit that I was confused by the first skill he taught me—how to fall. In my very first lesson, Ladi took me up what is now known as the Red Buffalo Express lift. On the way up, he explained to me that we were going to practice falling. *Is he serious? That doesn't sound like much fun.*

That was exactly what we did for much of my first lesson. "Falling is nothing to worry about" is one of Ladi's mottos in life. He believes the only thing that prevents most people from trying new things is fear. To eliminate that fear, according to Ladi, we must first learn how to fail.

Obviously, you can't stand back up unless you fall. Think about it: we learned to fall before we walked. When we fell as babies, we didn't stop trying to walk. We learned to catch ourselves, and before too long, we were running everywhere. We fall. We get back up. We learn. We grow. We live.

That first day, after learning to fall and roll, I discovered how to stand on my skis again. From that day forward, I didn't worry about falling anymore. Ladi taught me that falling wasn't as scary as I believed and that getting back up was even more rewarding than I ever could have imagined. I've tried to apply that mantra to everything I've attempted in life.

Over the years, I learned Ladi's story during my lessons, and it became evident to me that he was never afraid of falling or trying new things. He led a life of adventure from a young age and took many chances to reach his full potential and obtain the life he wanted. He wasn't afraid to fall over the edge and always hoped that what was over the horizon was more glorious than anything he had ever seen.

We fall. We get back up. We learn. We grow. We live.

Ladi was born in Czechoslovakia in August 1961, about thirteen years after the country had its last elected president and seven years before the Soviet Union awarded leadership to Alexander Dubček. His era of power became known as the "Prague Spring" because he was more liberal than his predecessors, giving the people of Czechoslovakia increased freedom of speech, including freedom of the press. In August 1968, when Ladi was just seven, the Soviets decided a more liberal Czechoslovakia was a threat and sent more than half a million troops into the country to squash student-led protests.[175]

Ladi grew up in the Czech city of Ostrava, located in the northeast corner of the country, about fifteen kilometers from the Polish border. When

Ladi lived there in the 1960s, it was heavily industrial because of its abundance of coal. His father, also named Ladislav, had one of the most dangerous jobs in the world—working with explosives in the mines. Ladi's brother, Jindra, followed his father's footsteps and also works as a mining blast technician. His mother, Vera, was a chef in a school for homeless children.

Ladi's life under communism was much simpler than what it is now in the United States. Some of his fondest memories of his childhood occurred when he was part of a group that was similar to the Boy Scouts of America. He went to summer camp for three weeks every year, which instilled a love for nature in him. He also spent many weekends at his grandmother's house, located near a small rail station. One day, a conductor asked him if he wanted to ride on a train, which piqued his interest in transportation.

In 1976, Ladi left home at age fifteen to attend a vocational school to learn how to become a train conductor. The boarding school that Ladi attended was located in Šumperk, which was at the foot of the Jeseníky Mountains. The school owned a ski resort, and students operated the chairlifts as a part of their education. Ladi and his classmates stayed in a cottage near the lifts. At midnight, it was a tradition to turn the lifts on and ski at least one run, with the leader showing everyone the way by holding a cucumber jar with a lit candle inside since they didn't have headlamps.

Šumperk is where Ladi became an exceptional skier. When his classmates tried to teach him how to ski moguls, he struggled to keep his skis together, which is the only way you can navigate your way through large snow-covered mounds with a series of sharp turns. As a solution, his classmates locked his skis together at the bindings with a padlock and pushed him down the trail. To watch him ski moguls now is like watching a performing artist dance down the mountain.

There was only one problem: within nine months of arriving at the boarding school, Ladi was on the verge of being expelled. He was drinking, smoking, skipping classes, and chasing girls.

One of Ladi's professors came to his rescue and told the headmaster, "If you give me a chance, I will fix this guy." The professor's decision to speak up and intervene changed Ladi's life. He told Ladi, "If you want to be part of the group that operates the ski resort, you need to change your behavior and take school seriously. You need to study. Only then can you be part of the ski team."

Ladi so much wanted to ski with his friends that he was the number one student in his class when he graduated four years later.

Although the Red Army occupied Šumperk while

Ladi was there, he and his friends were interested in many Western things, like rock music and hot dog skiing, the fearless style of downhill skiing that was popular in the United States at the time. He started a freestyle club at his school and helped raise money to build an additional cottage for club members. They participated in competitions and later organized the first freestyle skiing national championships in the Czech Republic. Ladi won the very first one.

Under communism, any male over eighteen years old had to serve a compulsory military service. Ladi had two options: if he studied at a university, he could take one day a week of military education, similar to ROTC training in the United States. If he followed that path, he could join the military at a higher rank and his required service would shorten by one year. The other option was going straight into the military and serving two years. Ladi decided to go to the university, and he picked a university that was close to the mountains of High Tatras in Slovakia. Computers were becoming popular by this time, and he was interested in how robotics related to transportation. He earned a bachelor's degree in computer science and robotics from the technical University of Zilina in 1985.

After finishing university, Ladi served as an air traffic controller for the Czech Air Force. He oversaw a squadron of fighter jets and planned missions.

Because of the Iron Curtain's reach, his radar stretched from the Mediterranean to the Baltic Sea.

It was a historic time in Ladi's homeland. In January 1989, two decades after a university student named Jan Palach climbed the steps of the National Museum in Prague, doused himself with gasoline, and lit a match in protest of the Soviet invasion, the underground efforts to overthrow the occupation were revealed. The clandestine movement to end communist rule in Czechoslovakia became known as the Velvet Revolution.

On November 17, 1989, eight days after the Berlin Wall fell in Germany, student protestors flocked to the streets of Prague:

> [T]he same tide of freedom that had swept Berlin seemed to have come to the Czech capital," according to *TIME*. "Police tried to beat back the demonstrators, hoping to tamp down the demand for freedom, but the people seemed to have grown immune to the brutality of the regime; the show of force only galvanized the resistance.
>
> The students were joined in the coming days by Czechoslovak citizens of all ages. By [November] 20, a half-million Czechs and Slovaks filled Prague's streets and took over Wenceslas Square. The Communists were

forced out. By the end of 1989, Czechoslovakia
was on its way to having an elected President
for the first time since 1948.[176]

After the Soviet Union fell, Ladi's military
obligation ended, and he worked as a computer
programmer for a company in Šumperk, which by
then he considered his home. Unfortunately, much of
the early computer coding and programs he worked
with were written in English. He had learned Czech
and Russian under communism, so he had to wait
for someone else to translate the English program-
ming manuals and literature.

In the summer of 1990, after Ladi had married
his wife, Martina, and they had their first daughter,
Jane, he decided to do something about his language
gap. He believed he could learn English in about six
weeks and persuaded his new wife to let him try.

Ladi took six weeks of vacation and hitchhiked
more than 1,400 kilometers to the United Kingdom.
After he and his friend crossed the English Channel
via a ferry, officers stopped them at customs. UK
officials asked Ladi why he was traveling. He told
them he was there to learn English. When they asked
how he was going to pay for his housing and food
in London, he told them he had saved about 300
pounds, which wasn't much.

Of course, customs officials assumed Ladi was

coming there to work without a visa. They searched his luggage and found a tourist's guide, which had one page in the entire book that detailed employment agencies. That was enough evidence to prove that he was trying to work illegally, according to UK customs, so the officers jailed Ladi and his university classmate, accusing them of trying to work without the proper documentation.

The next day, when an attorney interviewed Ladi and his friend, his classmate proved that he had enough money to cover expenses for both of them. Only then did officers release Ladi and his friend.

Ladi found a job as a kitchen porter at a restaurant, and nearly all of his salary went to pay for his tuition for language classes. He went to school in the morning and worked ten hours a day at the restaurant. Ladi only ate when he was working. If he wasn't needed at work on weekends, he often didn't eat because he didn't have money to pay for food. Over time, his bosses promoted him to fry cook and then grill chef at the restaurant, so he made more money.

Ladi was given permission to stay in London longer, and, eventually, Martina and Jane were able to join him in London, and his wife helped support his education by working as a nanny. Ladi continued to work full-time in the restaurant while also taking daily classes to study English, and after nine months he passed an exam of Cambridge Certificate of

Proficiency in English. It took him longer than he'd anticipated, but as he likes to say, you can't walk before you learn to fall.

Because of his interest in computers and transportation, Ladi wanted to continue studying in London. He went to the Czech embassy and asked about applying for a scholarship. Czech officials told Ladi that he could apply with the caveat that the chances of being awarded a scholarship were close to nil; he applied nevertheless. Then, a few months later, the embassy called and told him a scholarship had opened up. It was supposed to go to a son of a high-ranking government official, but the boy had failed his English proficiency test.

Ladi ended up getting the scholarship to attend the London School of Economics, where he earned a master's degree in operations research in about a year. His studies eventually took him to America, where he studied at the Georgia Institute of Technology in Atlanta and Cornell University in Ithaca, New York.

Despite all of his moving around, Ladi was never far from the ski slopes. While he attended Cornell, he coached the ski team at Greek Peak Mountain Resort in Cortland, New York. His daughter, Jane, was on the team and became one of the top female skiers on the East Coast. Her progress caused Ladi to relocate his family to Vail, Colorado, so she would have greater opportunities in the sport. By then, Ladi and Martina had another daughter, Kiki, and a son, Dominik.

In November 2003, Ladi approached Beaver Creek Resort about becoming a ski instructor. During preseason training, another instructor asked Ladi if he could help him with a double booking over the Christmas holidays. I was that client. I ended up skiing with Ladi every winter ever since. By the time I was

You can't walk before you learn to fall.

a teenager, he became one of my closest friends and, as I said earlier, one of my most influential mentors.

Unfortunately, I am no longer officially one of Ladi's clients because we were caught skiing out of bounds unintentionally. The ski school fired Ladi for the transgression. When they called my parents and told them that they had identified a new instructor for me, Mom and Dad said I only wanted to ski with Ladi. We've continued to share our passion for playing in the outdoors for years to come.

One of our favorite activities to do together is Swiss bobsledding. We know of a hiking trail in the woods that has become sort of a bobsled run because so many people have walked through it. Our "bobsled" is actually a light plastic sled with two handles, which we throw over our shoulders for the three-mile hike to the top of the run. We can get four people in the sled, tied together like a train, and it's so much fun.

We go bobsledding after a long day of skiing, so it's often dark by the time we reach the top of the pass, and we have to use headlamps to see as we sled down. One night while hiking, Ladi received a text message that a young man who was snowboarding in Beaver Creek had been reported missing. Ladi was a member of the Vail Mountain Search and Rescue team and had experience from going on many rescue missions. Within a short time of receiving the missing person report, we heard someone calling for help, and we followed the sound and found a young boy in a deep snow well. He was buried headfirst in the snow and couldn't reach the bindings on his snowboard to release himself. If we hadn't found him that night, he might have become a popsicle and frozen to death by morning. Ladi then called the search and rescue mission coordinator, who notified the young man's father that his son had been found safe and that we would escort him to the trailhead parking lot where we witnessed happy tears of the father-son reunion.

Remember what Ladi said about learning to fall? Sometimes your ability to do it can be the difference between life and death!

Ladi likes to say our relationship is a two-way street. I've learned so much from him about skiing, hiking, ice climbing, mountain climbing (more on that later), kayaking, mountain biking, and bobsledding. Ladi says I've taught him about overcoming adversity because I've never once complained to him about my medical problems. He says I've also taught him about being grateful for everything life gives you, especially the encounters you have with other people. I'm not sure I agree with him, but Ladi says he has learned as much from me as he has taught me.

One of the attributes I respect most about Ladi is that he never stops learning. Whether it's fly-fishing, endurance racing, cooking, or hunting, Ladi is determined to try to learn new things. He's a big believer in being exposed to as many things as possible and being well-rounded. He believes there's something to be learned, no matter how small, in everything you try. And, of course, he believes you learn by falling.

What have you been afraid to try? What's holding you back from your next adventure? Failure is simply a stepping-stone on your way to success. Of course, this doesn't mean that failure is easy to deal with or that it should be taken lightly, but how you deal with failure will determine both your future successes and also how easily those can be achieved. Everyone has different coping mechanisms and ways they react to failure. However, learning the ways that more often lead you to success can help you enormously!

Always remember to learn from your failures,

Failure is simply a stepping-stone on your way to success.

put your head down and forge ahead, and set goals that are attainable. Most importantly, surround yourself with good people. Just keep trying. It's likely that you can think of someone you know who set his or her mind on a goal and would stop at nothing to achieve it. It's not just some kind of story or fantasy—this could be *you* too! Adopt this drive and apply it to your situation. When you believe in yourself and your abilities, you'll gain the motivation to keep moving forward, and you'll feel unstoppable.

The most important thing I've learned is that God will get you back on your feet. Don't be afraid to fall. Just get back up. If you fall behind, get back in front. If you fall down, get back up. If you fall off, get back on. Don't stop falling or trying. There's nothing more rewarding than putting yourself back together. Trust me, after everything I've endured in my life, I would know.

CHAPTER TWELVE

Leave the Nest

DURING THE LAST few years, a story about bald eagles has been passed around the internet over and over again. Many of the people who have read it probably assume it is true because, well, everything that's published on the internet is perceived to be true these days—no matter the source.

A man in India supposedly wrote the story about the eagle. It goes like this:

> The Eagle has the longest life span of its species. It can live up to seventy years.
>
> But to reach this age, the eagle must make a very difficult decision!
>
> In its 40th year, the eagle's long and flexible talons can no longer grab a prey which serves as food.
>
> Its long and sharp beak becomes bent.
>
> Its old-aged and heavy wings, due to their thick feathers, stick to its chest and make it difficult to fly.[177]

At that point, according to the author, an eagle has two options, neither of which is very inviting: it can die of starvation or it can endure a thoroughly painful five-month process in which it sits in a nest high in the mountains and bangs its beak against a rock until it breaks off. Then the bald eagle must wait for a new beak to grow so it can pluck out its old and heavy wings, which will eventually be replaced by new ones.

"And after this, the eagle takes its famous flight of rebirth and LIVES for 30 more years," the author wrote.

Now, in case you didn't already know, let me point out a couple of fundamental problems with the story. First and foremost, bald eagles typically live about twenty-eight years in the wild (not seventy) according to *National Geographic*.[178] Second, an eagle's beak and talons are made of keratin, the same material of our fingernails.[179] The beak isn't growing back overnight! And, finally, wouldn't the bald eagle die of starvation while waiting for its new beak and feathers to grow back anyhow? It can't kill and eat without a beak, and it can't fly to locate prey without feathers. Is it ordering room service or Uber Eats while it waits?

Obviously, the story isn't true, like a lot of other things you will find on the World Wide Web. But the reason I mentioned the story is that I appreciate the central point the author attempts to drive home through his not-so-factual tale about the legendary American symbol—that we need change in order to thrive. "We sometimes need to get rid of the unpleasant old memories, negative habits and our fixed mindset. . . . In order to take on a New Journey ahead, let go of your negative old limiting beliefs. Open up your mind and let yourself fly high like an eagle!"[180]

Now, I'm not telling you to pry off your fingernails or pluck every hair from your head. I'm only saying that at some point in our lives, we each have to fly from the nest, accept change gracefully, and adapt to our new surroundings. We have to take chances and listen to our guts when making difficult choices.

In August 2004, I made that bold move to leave the nest when I left the comfortable surroundings of my parents' home for High Point University in North Carolina. For the first time in my life, I was going to be alone to stand up for myself and fight for the accommodations I would need to be a successful college student.

Of course, there were still going to be plenty of people there to support me. At High Point, every freshman is assigned to a life coach, and mine was a wonderful man named Akir Khan, who had worked in the George W. Bush administration as a liaison to the Muslim community before joining High Point, where he was working toward a doctorate in educational leadership.

In our first meeting, Dr. Khan told me, "I want you to know I'll always have your back, JT. I've experienced similar things. For example, I had bad enough asthma that I couldn't be in sports or join the military like I wanted to. I never let it stop me, but it was hard. That's why I'm thrilled today to be a mentor to students and help them develop their game plans."

I met with Dr. Khan once a week and eventually he told me that I had what he called a growth mindset, which is an ability to adapt to situations and a willingness to be uncomfortable in order to learn outside the box and evolve. If he only knew how much I was used to being uncomfortable!

As I told you earlier, Mom and Dad were my biggest advocates when I was younger, but I assumed the role for myself in high school and would need to do so even more in college. Eventually, my parents taught me to stand on my own. They told me to take ownership of my struggles and problems and learn how to solve them. They gave me additional responsibilities as I grew older, and they talked through potential solutions when I couldn't figure things out. At High Point, it was up to me, not my parents, to ask for accommodations because of my learning differences, and the university and its faculty and staff weren't going to offer them without me first asking.

According to Understood, an organization dedicated to individuals with thinking and learning differences, "Colleges don't fall under the Individuals with Disabilities Education Act, which is why there are no IEPs" like in high school.[181] But most colleges have a disability services office for students with learning and thinking differences, and I worked with employees in that office to come up with a plan for how I could succeed at High Point. At the beginning of my first semester as a freshman, my accommodations letter stated that I could record the lectures in class. I could also request copies of lecture notes. I was permitted to use alternative versions of textbooks, such as audio recordings, which I used while I read. For exams, I was able to take the tests in a distraction-reduced room, could use software that read the exam to me and recorded my oral responses, and I was afforded more time to complete the work.

My parents taught me to stand on my own. They told me to take ownership of my struggles and problems and learn how to solve them.

I will admit that these accommodations were the difference in me passing or failing every course that

I took during my four years at High Point. Some of the faculty went out of their way to help me complete my work despite my short-term memory and reading issues, and I will forever be grateful and thankful for their dedication, empathy, and kindness.

For example, Dr. Kara Dixon Vuic, the professor in my first history course, American Aspirations, came to understand that I had difficulties getting my answers and ideas down on paper. So Dr. Vuic made arrangements for me to come to class early when we were having a test or quiz, and then stayed with me afterward to go through my answers orally to make sure I was getting my point across.

However, some of my professors wouldn't budge when it came to certain rules, although they were kind to me when they explained their reasoning. For instance, High Point didn't allow anyone to use calculators on math tests—period. Without a calculator, I bombed my first big math test. I conferred with my Learning Excellence academic coach, Heather Slocum, who helped me request to use a calculator in a revised accommodations letter. But when I approached the math professor with the letter, she still wouldn't change her mind.

Through these trials and struggles, I earned a deeper awareness of what I can and cannot do well and how to compensate for my shortcomings. At times, it was extremely stressful, but I ultimately learned a valuable lesson. I was out of the nest and comforts of my home for the first time, but I was determined to advocate for myself.

Fortunately, I had a wide support system in place. Julie Martin Kelly, my tutor from home, was still working with me. She had copies of my textbooks and assignments and helped me break down the material and concentrate on what I needed to know. She also helped me tremendously with time management and learning how to study properly and efficiently. We met via Skype four times each week, and working with her provided me with the confidence I needed to pass my classes and juggle everything on my plate.

The Learning Excellence office, including Suzanne Hawks, Craig Curty, and Pamala Wannamaker, helped me keep my head up when I struggled with a lesson or didn't do well on a test. Mrs. Slocum helped me create weekly to-do lists and calendars, and she reviewed material with me.

Even though I received help from many different people who truly cared about me and very much wanted me to succeed, I also came to realize that I had to learn the material, understand it, and do the work on my own. Ultimately, it was up to me to put in the necessary time and effort to pass my classes, regardless of whatever accommodations and assistance I was receiving.

At the time, I was reminded of a column that my mother had shared with me a few years earlier. Kendra Graham, a Bible teacher and the wife of the evangelist Will Graham, was the author. Doctors had diagnosed one of their children with dyslexia in the second grade. She compared her daughter's learning disability to the formation of a pearl:

> A pearl is formed in an oyster because of an irritation that finds its way to the inside of the shell. The oyster wraps the irritation with a coat of mother of pearl. The larger the irritation, the more coats of this substance are used to wrap around the point of pain until, in the end, the irritation is gone, but a beautiful, costly pearl is formed. Often the things for which we have to work hardest are the things we treasure the most.[182]

Graham wrote that her daughter had to work harder than Graham's other children. Assignments that should have taken ten minutes took an hour or more to complete. Like me, her daughter has to learn something and then learn it again and again until it gets "stuck" in her brain. Graham watched her daughter get mad and frustrated and wondered, *Why her? Why not me?*[183]

One day, as Graham and her daughter worked

through an assignment that was taking much longer than it should have, Graham decided to simply complete the work herself. Her daughter glanced up and said, "Don't steal my pearl! It's my treasure!" Reflecting on this conversation, Graham wrote, "Letting our children struggle is hard, but God has entrusted this testimony to my daughter. I can stand beside her and support her, but the battle is hers—as is the treasure."[184]

After all my trials and tribulations, after all my hard work and the help from so many others who loved me, raised me up along the way, and encouraged me to do my best, my pearl came in the form of a bachelor's of science in business administration degree from High Point University. I graduated with a GPA of 3.21. I had left the nest and achieved this victory on my own.

Of course, my mother and father were there to see me get my diploma, along with both sets of my grandparents, when I walked across the stage at the promenade in the center of

"Often the things for which we have to work hardest are the things we treasure the most."

the High Point campus on May 5, 2018. The singer-actor-philanthropist Josh Groban delivered the commencement speech, the first of his life, on that very muggy day. His speech truly pulled at my heart; he talked about change, taking chances, and risks.[185]

Groban grew up in Los Angeles and first performed in the seventh grade.[186] He attended the Los Angeles County School for the Arts as a theatre major. He enrolled at Carnegie Mellon University in Pittsburgh, where he planned to study theatre.[187] Only a few months into his first semester, however, a studio offered him a recording deal.

"I'm thinking back to when I was sitting on my dorm bed after getting that fateful call and wondering, *Should I stay in the program?*" Groban told us that day. "*Follow the dotted line I decided for myself, even with this sudden golden door swinging open before me?* I was going to be a theater graduate and do my showcase and slowly work my way to Broadway. That was the path I had planned. But I got offered a chance for a recording career by a major label."[188]

On one hand, Groban was offered an amazing opportunity in the form of a major record deal. On the other, there was tremendous risk. He would have to drop out of college to do it, and that would require him to leave the nest in an entirely different way than he had planned. It was a life-altering decision that would require him to abandon the plans he had made for his life. Plus, at the time, the top-selling artists in the United States included names such as Britney Spears, TLC, Garth Brooks, and the Backstreet Boys. He hardly fit into those genres.

"I was the farthest from a sure thing marketing-wise as you could get—but what a chance. A risk, but a great chance," he said. "I didn't know what to do. I remembered something a camp counselor told me. Flip a coin, flip it high, and while it's in the air, you'll get a sense of what you really want, how you want it to land. It's the gut check."

Groban went with his gut, packed his bag, and signed the record deal. He took a chance and embraced change.

"If my noncollege education has taught me anything, it's how easy it is to get tripped up by the word *should*," Groban told us. "You should do this. This is the way it should be done. And it's not just other people to tell you that. The biggest voice is your own."[189]

The most amazing thing about Josh Groban's story is that he was terrified of singing when he was a kid. Groban knew he could sing, but he would close his door, put on his headphones, and sing Nirvana and show tunes to an audience of one. Finally, in the seventh grade, he mustered the courage to join the choir. His voice was changing because of puberty, but the choir teacher recognized something in him and gave him a lofty assignment: to learn a George Gershwin song entitled "'S Wonderful," and sing it in front of the school on their cabaret night. Groban was terrified but practiced singing the song each night. "That risk, it changed my life," he said. "It led to more singing, eventually getting lead roles in high school."[190]

During his commencement speech, Groban recalled an incident in 1999 when David Foster, "one of the most influential music producers and writers in the world," called him and asked him to fill in for the great Italian opera singer Andrea Bocelli in a rehearsal for the GRAMMYs—with Celine Dion! Amazingly, Groban told Foster that he didn't want to do it. He didn't know the song, and it was in Italian. Bocelli was one of the world's most famous tenors; Groban was a young lyric baritone.

A few minutes after their call ended, Foster called Groban back. He had already been working with Groban and had recognized his enormous potential. He knew it was an opportunity that Groban couldn't pass up. He said, "Get your [rear] over here. I'm not asking you, I'm telling you. I'll see you in six hours."

In the end, once Groban calmed his nerves, he killed the duet with Celine Dion. It was so good that she invited him to sing the song with her again on a TV special. He recorded his own version of the song on his debut album, which went six times platinum.

He even sang the song with Bocelli at the GRAMMYs ten years later.[191]

"You're all here because of your incredibly hard work and effort and beautiful minds," Groban told us. "But you're also here because someone helped. . . . Think of someone who did that for you, anyone who along the way gave you that push, made you take stock, helped you find your path and your voice, or encouraged you to take a risk, that said the uncomfortable thing for your benefit."[192]

As I sat in the audience with my fellow 2018 High Point University graduates that day, I thought of all the people who had helped me reach that milestone in my life: my parents, grandparents, friends, doctors, surgeons, nurses, mentors, reading tutors, teachers, counselors, professors, and anyone else who had made a huge impact in my life. They pushed me along the way, made me believe that I could accomplish anything I wanted, and helped me find my voice and path—the one that God had chosen for me. In my heart, I knew it was His plan for me all along. I was reminded of Isaiah 41:10:

> So do not fear, for I am with you;
>   do not be dismayed, for I am your God.
> I will strengthen you and help you;
>   I will uphold you with my righteous right hand.

> *I thought of all the people who had helped me reach that milestone in my life. . . . They pushed me along the way, made me believe that I could accomplish anything I wanted, and helped me find my voice and path—the one that God had chosen for me.*

Near the end of his commencement speech, Groban admitted that he still has fears like the rest of us. Some of his albums haven't connected with listeners, and some of his TV shows weren't successful. People in the media and others on social media have criticized him.[193]

I'm guessing that he still made the right decision that day in his dorm room at Carnegie Mellon. He has released many multiplatinum albums and has sold millions of records worldwide. He was cast in the TV shows *The Office* and *Ally McBeal* and the film

Crazy, Stupid, Love. He has performed on Broadway and been nominated for a Tony Award for best actor. He's doing okay for a college dropout.

"The good news is people won't really pay as much attention to your missteps as you do, especially if they were in the name of moving forward and growth," he said. "You will make them, and you will be challenged to pick yourself up when you do."[194]

Change is hard, Groban warned us, and we have to remember to rely on our gut feelings. At the end of the speech, he sang a few lines from one of his favorite songs as a child, Stephen Sondheim's "Move On."

> Stop worrying where you're going.
>   Move on.
> If you can know where you're going,
>   you've gone.
> Just keep moving on.[195]

After we walked onto the stage, one by one, and received our diplomas and shook hands with Groban and Dr. Qubein that day, it was time for a High Point University tradition. At the end of every graduation, an eagle—the symbol of freedom and strength and pride—is untethered to fly high above the thousands of people who are sitting on the promenade lawn.

That day, on that lawn, the eagle wasn't the only one soaring.

CHAPTER THIRTEEN

Pole, Pole

....

AS A KID, I used to love flipping through the *Guinness World Records* books to read about the absolutely insane things people did to distinguish themselves as world record holders. Since 1955,[196] *Guinness World Records*, which started as a promotion for Guinness Brewery to settle pub arguments,[197] has documented more than 53,000 world records in its database and adds about 8,000 new ones every year.[198]

Some of the world records recorded by Guinness are truly bizarre. Recently it added the following accomplishments:

- Farthest arrow shot using feet: 40 feet, 4.64 inches (by Brittany Walsh of the United States)[199]
- Most toothpicks in a beard: 3,500 (by Joel Strasser of the United States)[200]
- Highest jump on a pogo stick: 11.15 feet (by Dmitry Arsenyev of Russia)[201]
- Longest hair on a teenager: 6 feet, 6.7 inches (by Nilanshi Patel of India)[202]
- Largest hula hoop spun by a female: 17 feet, 0.25 inches in diameter (by Getti Kehayova of the United States)[203]

- Most consecutive pinky pull-ups: 36 (by Tazio Gavioli of Italy)[204]
- Fastest time to eat a bowl of pasta: 26.69 seconds (by Michelle Lesco of the United States)[205]

A few of them are bizarre, right? That's why I was so surprised that the Guinness record management team rejected my application for a world record in December 2019.

I'll admit that my world record—Guinness might not recognize it yet, but I'm holding out hope that it one day will—is a little bit out there. I didn't pierce my body 462 times like Elaine Davidson of the United Kingdom,[206] nor did I eat 28,788 Big Macs in my life like Donald Gorske of the United States,[207] and I didn't spend over a thousand hours getting tattoos like Lucky Diamond Rich of New Zealand.[208] However, I'm certain my world record would be one of the most unusual ones in the book.

Before I tell you about the record, let me first share with you the story behind it. About five months after I graduated from High Point University, I wanted to complete one of the most challenging items on my bucket list—climbing Mount Kilimanjaro.

Kili, as the Tanzanians refer to it, is a dormant volcano that is believed to have formed about 750,000 years ago through eruptions.[209] It actually has three volcanic cones: Kibo, Mawenzi, and Shira. Mawenzi and Shira are extinct, but Kibo, the tallest, is dormant and might erupt again. We were headed to the highest point at Uhuru Peak, located on the outer crater rim of Kibo.[210]

Of course, to accomplish one of the most challenging climbing feats in the world, I knew I would need help from my friend Ladi Lettovsky and his wife, Martina. Ladi did much of the planning for our expedition, booking airline tickets with his myriad points, choosing our licensed commercial guide (which is a requirement of the Tanzanian government), locating our hotels, and making sure we would be fully equipped with everything we needed once we arrived.

On October 2, 2018, we flew from Denver to Miami—already wearing our hiking boots. Then we took an eight-hour red-eye flight to Heathrow Airport in London, where Ladi introduced me to potato pancakes and something called black pudding. My breakfast was followed by a nearly nine-hour flight to Nairobi and another shorter flight to Kilimanjaro.

After traveling for thirty-three hours and going through customs in Tanzania, we finally arrived at our hotel at three o'clock in the morning. Fortunately, I am able to sleep on the planes because we were scheduled to wake up four hours later to begin our climb.

Since we were already acclimated to higher elevations in Colorado, Ladi wanted us to start the climb right away and not rest in the town of Moshi, which has an elevation of 3,120 feet.

Our guide, Simon Mtuy, the founder and director of Summit Expeditions & Nomadic Experience, greeted us at our hotel that morning. I liked Simon and his assistant guide, Manase Lyimo, immediately.

Simon is a Chagga tribesman who grew up in a small village in the shadows of Kili. He was the fifth of ten children in a poor family. His first job at fourteen was to porter equipment for international climbers up the peak. He became a licensed guide at twenty-one.[211] Simon estimates he has been to the top of Kili more than three hundred times, according to his company's website.[212]

Simon is also one of the world's foremost trail runners. In 2006, he established a Guinness world record for the fastest unsupported ascent/descent of Mount Kilimanjaro. He went up and back down the mountain in only nine hours, twenty-one minutes.[213] In 2010, Spanish skyrunning athlete Kílian Jornet Burgada broke Simon's record by ascending and descending Kili in seven hours, fourteen minutes— after Simon trained him![214]

Simon completed the unsupported climb/ descent—in which you are required to carry your own equipment, water, and supplies—in part to raise money for his three young nephews and nieces. His brother, Joechikim, died of AIDS in 2004, leaving the children behind. Simon wanted to raise money to support their education and bring awareness to the HIV/AIDS epidemic in the villages surrounding the mountain.[215] He hoped to build a community center in memory of his brother, where he could help train AIDS widows and provide education about the disease.[216]

In 2019, according to the HIV education charity Avert, Tanzania had 1.7 million people living with HIV. There were 77,000 new HIV infections that year and 27,000 AIDS-related deaths.[217]

Simon is the director of the NGO Hope Through Opportunity in Tanzania, which aims to curtail HIV transmission and provide independence and stability to youth and women in the villages at the foothills of Kili. Simon is also an advocate for environmental sustainability and conservation in the region.[218]

The morning we arrived in Tanzania, we took a winding dirt road through villages and coffee and banana plantations to reach the gates of Mount Kilimanjaro National Park. When I saw the mountain for the first time, it was as if Kili was floating in the mist and dark, gray clouds. Because of the snow on its peak, the ancient Chagga believed Kili was the seat of God.[219] Indeed, the rooftop of Africa was mysterious and awe inspiring—and, of course, massive.

After filling our water bottles and CamelBaks, we were introduced to our team of fifteen porters. In yet another humanitarian effort, Simon has worked to bring attention to the mistreatment of porters, who in the past have died on the mountain from hypothermia, altitude sickness, and exhaustion. Some of them weren't even wearing shoes and didn't have proper clothing and gear. That is one of the reasons porters are only allowed to carry luggage that weighs 32 pounds or less up the mountain.[220]

Our porters were strong, hardworking people, some of whom only spoke Swahili. They carried everything we didn't, including tents, food, water, and even a portable toilet. Quite a few of them made multiple trips up and down the mountain during our expedition to supply us with fresh food. We appreciated their hard work and respected them deeply.

Ladi had an ambitious plan for our climb. It takes most people seven or eight days to get up and down Kili. Ladi wanted us to do it in only four! With Simon's guidance, we were also taking the least traveled and most difficult trek up the mountain—the Umbwe route. It's a shorter, steeper, and a more direct climb from the southern part of the mountain.[221]

One Kili guide company estimates the success rate for climbers on the Umbwe route is only 60 to 70 percent. It's about 85 percent for climbers who take seven days on the Machame route and about

90 percent for those who take eight days on the Lemosho route.[222] Overall, climbers taking only five days (or less) on any of the six routes up Kili have a success rate of only 27 percent![223]

This is a description (or warning) of the Umbwe route from one of the other guide services: "The Umbwe route has a well-deserved reputation of being the most challenging route on Mount Kilimanjaro. Due to the fast ascent to high altitude, this route does not provide the necessary stages for acclimatization. Although the number of people on this trail is very low, the chances of success are also low. Umbwe is considered to be [a] very difficult, taxing route—one that should only be attempted by strong hikers who are confident in their ability to acclimatize quickly to altitude."[224]

Since we had spent months preparing for our Mount Kilimanjaro climb in Colorado, Ladi was confident we could handle it. Making our climb even more difficult, Ladi and Simon had planned for us to start on Umbwe and then cut over to traverse what is known as the Western Breach. "A Kilimanjaro ascent via the Western Breach route is the most challenging and also by far the most dangerous way to scale Kibo and reach Uhuru Peak," one description of the route says. "The danger lies not in the climb itself, it lies in the melting glaciers above the route. As the glaciers retreat they release previously bound up rocks."[225]

On January 4, 2006, a group of Americans were climbing from Arrow Glacier Camp to the Western Breach when a sudden rockslide, estimated to have been traveling at more than 125 feet per second, killed three of them. Another climber and four porters were badly injured. Kibo's receding ice was believed to be the cause of the rockslide, and as a result of the tragedy, authorities changed the route to minimize climbers' exposure to the rocks in what became known as the "death zone."[226]

Boy, I sure hope my parents and grandparents aren't reading this.

On the first day of the climb, we hiked nearly seven miles and climbed from 5,382 feet to 9,356 feet above sea level. The muddy route took us through a natural rain forest, where we encountered colobus and blue monkeys in the trees. We encountered only one other hiker, a woman who was alone.

At times, the trek was steep, and I had to use tree roots as steps and ladders. Eventually, the path narrowed and steepened as we climbed the ridge between the Lonzo and Umbwe Rivers. Enormous trees surrounded us, and we had to use our hiking poles a lot. Finally, we ended our hike at Umbwe Cave Camp, where I did a treatment lying on my back in my tent. It was still an inconvenience for me, but at least I no longer had to sit in a bathroom for hours at a time. I was able to wait until the end of my day, so it wasn't as much of a burden as when I was a kid. Using a carabiner, I hooked a bag of my solution to the top of the inside of my tent. It was cold in my tent that first night, but nothing like what would be coming.

Pole, pole—pronounced po-lay, po-lay—means "slowly, slowly" in Swahili. For the porters and guides who have ascended and descended Kili myriad times, it means much more than that. Quite simply, it means less is more. By taking fewer, slower steps, you will get to the top and do it faster—even if it takes you longer. If you try to sprint to the summit, you'll undoubtedly be injured, suffer altitude sickness, or even worse. By conserving our energy, we ensured that we would have plenty of stamina, energy, and strength to complete our mission. *Pole, pole* means putting one foot in front of the other slowly.

Or as Simon says on his company's website, "*Pole pole* is also the way of life in Tanzania ('no hurry in Africa!') as people understand the value of taking life slowly, savoring the moment, the people, and the place where you are here and now. Westerners are only beginning to adopt this 'slow' mentality in some areas of our life in order to combat the 24/7 non-stop wired and electronically tethered world that drives us crazy but we can't seem to get away from. Yes, we are deeply connected, but that connection is filtered through a device to the virtual community. Slow connectedness is relating to those people, places, and events in the immediate world that surround you—connected to the 'here and now.'"[227]

Even though our quest to reach Uhuru Peak and back in four days might have been converse to *pole, pole*, Simon and his assistant guides encouraged us to move slowly and appreciate our surroundings and God's beauty the entire way.

Our second day climbing the mountain wasn't as long as the first, but it was much steeper and more challenging. I spent much of my time walking with Martina, while Ladi walked ahead at his own pace. We had exited the dense rainforest and entered the climate zone known as the heath/moorland. It has rocky terrain, sparse undergrowth, and straggly, moss-covered trees. Some of the moss hung over the trail like spiderwebs.

When the trail came up to a slight ridge, we spotted Mount Meru, forty miles away, in a sea of thick clouds. It's Tanzania's second-highest peak. Along the route, we scrambled around rocks in a field of boulders. When we reached the sheer, exposed Umbwe ridge, we could see valleys and hear rushing water. A little while later, we finally caught a glimpse of Kilimanjaro, blue and white and rising majestically on the horizon.

We hiked almost four miles, rising nearly 3,700 feet, on the second day. We stopped at Barranco Camp, situated in the valley beneath the Breach and Great Barranco Wall, which is 843 feet high. At just over 13,000 feet, I was amazed at the beauty of the landscape. I felt so close to God up there.

While waiting for dinner, I wanted to call my parents on my cell phone to let them know we had reached our stopping point. However, my phone had no connection. Neither did Martina's. We found Ladi high up on a rock with one bar of service. We joined him and called our families on speakerphone, letting them know we were safe and having the time of our lives.

By taking fewer, slower steps, you will get to the top and do it faster—even if it takes you longer.

The majestic sunset at dusk was more beautiful than anything I'd ever seen. With clouds above and below us, it was as if God had covered a giant canvas in brilliant hues of radiant orange and red. I was so at peace as the sun dropped below the clouds. I felt as if He had painted the sky only for me.

As I climbed into my tent for another cold night, I couldn't wait for the sun to rise the next morning. We were turning west and then north to climb another 1,500 feet higher than my highest previous elevation—Mount Elbert in Colorado.

Early the next morning, our guides awakened me to check my vitals in order to create a baseline of my breathing rate and oxygen saturation. When we'd started the hike two days earlier, I was breathing around sixteen breaths per minute. As we went higher, it rose to twenty, thirty, and then forty. When we reached the summit, I was warned, I would probably be sucking oxygen at fifty breaths a minute. The guides read the oxygen saturation in my blood with an instrument called a pulse oximeter, clipped on the end of my finger. The "pulse ox" used an infrared light to measure how red my blood was. Blood cells that aren't carrying enough oxygen are blue. Normal rates are 95 to 100 percent.[228]

As we climbed higher, there would be less oxygen in the air. If we didn't get enough oxygen, we might develop altitude sickness. The only previous time I had climbed this high, I had gotten sick. I was determined not to let it happen again.

Before breakfast, Martina asked me how I was doing. She and Ladi had already determined that there were three levels of "good" for me. Level 1 was, "Yes, JT is good." Level 2 was, "I don't feel so good." Level 3 was, "Help!" No matter how I felt, I typically told them I was "good," so this system was their own way of looking out for me. Fortunately,

Martina worked as a registered nurse in Colorado. Her medical expertise was going to come in handy before our climb was over.

We left Barranco Camp and climbed along a river with waterfalls and rose from moorland terrain into the arid brown alpine desert. Most climbers head south through the Karanga Valley and join up with the Mweka route to circle around and approach Uhuru Peak from the south. Instead, we were going to climb in the opposite direction, past Lava Tower Camp

The majestic sunset at dusk was more beautiful than anything I'd ever seen. . . . I felt as if He had painted the sky only for me.

and then north to Arrow Glacier and the dangerous Western Breach.

It got colder as we climbed, and when we reached the ridge we were aiming for, I glanced down at my altimeter hooked to the shoulder strap of my daypack. It read 14,439 feet—the exact altitude of the highest peak I'd been on at Mount Elbert!

We continued to follow Simon's lead of *pole,*

pole. But as we got closer to our destination, Arrow Glacier Camp at the foot of the foreboding Western Breach, I was starting to feel pressure in my head. I prepared myself for the inevitability that I would probably suffer altitude sickness the next day. I knew I'd have to stay hydrated, fueled up, and keep plenty of Advil in my pocket. That night, the cook, Christopher Agga, made us dinner, and Ladi handed me a helmet, which I would have to wear while climbing the Western Breach.

That night, I went to sleep earlier than usual because we were starting extremely early the next day—around four o'clock in the morning. It was the day I had dreamed about for so long: summit day! I hoped my stomach and head wouldn't prevent me from reaching the top of Kili.

The Western Breach is so dangerous that Simon won't guide climbers up that route anymore—at least that's what his company's website says.[229] I guess Ladi, as usual, was persuasive. The Western Breach, as its name suggests, is a gap on the western outer rim of Kili's main summit, Kibo. Lava flow formed it hundreds of thousands of years ago, which caused a massive collapse of part of the summit. Thick layers of ice—not as much as in the past—coat the high rim, binding geologic debris into place.[230]

As I said, as snow melts and recedes at the summit, rocks the size of SUVs can come bounding down the mountain. The last known death on the Western Breach was in 2015 when a falling boulder struck and killed thirty-two-year-old Scott Dinsmore, who died instantly. He was climbing the mountain with his wife, who was not injured. They had been taking a yearlong trip around the world and had visited twenty countries before climbing Kili.[231]

When I woke up at four o'clock the next day, I felt good, even if ice was covering the inside of my tent. My headache was gone, and I felt well rested. Manase took my vitals, and my oxygen level was sufficient. I had a warm breakfast of hot oatmeal and raisins, full of iron, which was good for my blood at altitudes that high. We filled our water bottles with a mixture of cold and hot water so they wouldn't freeze. I strapped on my helmet and headlamp and was ready to go.

Simon went over our planned route with us one more time, and a handful of the porters descended for supplies. The remaining ones would stay with us and carry emergency oxygen and medical equipment. We departed Arrow Glacier Camp at 5:26 a.m. and headed east-southeast—and straight up.

Back home, my parents were nervously following our progress on my website. My Garmin GPS posted a little dot every thirty minutes to show them where we were on a digital topography map. They watched as we slowly reached 16,029 feet, 16,518 feet, 16,885 feet, and so on.

We had to be exceptionally careful crossing the steep snowfields in the dark. *Pole, pole* was never more important. One false step could send one of us sliding thousands of feet below. We used our ice picks and hiking poles to make each step. Crossing the Western Breach in the dark might seem crazy, but falling rocks were less likely in subfreezing temperatures. It was paramount that we cross the danger zone before daybreak, so here we were following Simon with only the light from our headlamps.

After a couple of hours of climbing, we had crossed the Western Breach and stopped at an outcropping of boulders to catch our breath. Here, Simon delivered a warning: "My friends, we are at the point of no turning back."

Simon said it would be too difficult to climb back down once we started our ascent on the Rock Steps, our next challenge. Even if one of us was badly injured, the only way down was to continue up an additional five hundred feet into the crater and then cross it for a mile to begin our descent to the nearest camp.[232]

I glanced at Ladi. He glanced at Martina. They both turned and glanced at me. We were all smiling. There was no way we were turning back now. We were so close!

Only fifteen minutes later, I was second-guessing my decision. Immediately above us was a false summit. From a distance, it looked like the top of Kili. Once we got there, however, there was another ridge with more terrain beyond it. We kept climbing.

Then my stomach started to cramp with hot pain. It felt like it was boiling. A wave of nausea hit me. I was in pain but pushed on without telling Ladi and Martina. I knew I had to get to a toilet—as soon as possible!

My upset stomach was the result of a bug, which I believed I'd probably gotten from untreated water. Because of my compromised intestinal system, I also was starting to feel signs of altitude sickness. The summit was two hours away. Would I get so ill that Simon and Manase would have to carry me to the top? Worse, in my mind, would Ladi and Martina have to sacrifice their dream of getting there because of me?

Fortunately for me, as I mentioned earlier, Martina is a registered nurse and knew what to do immediately. She worked to keep me hydrated and started me on antibiotics.

In the now-blinding sunlight, we finally crawled over the rocky Western Breach rim into Kibo's caldera. A stunning, white, mile-wide expanse greeted us. We started climbing a rock field up many ridges toward Kibo's wall-high Furtwängler Glacier, or what was left of the ice cap that once covered all of Kilimanjaro.

We still had an hour to go, and we were getting tired. Fighting my exhaustion, I pushed behind Simon, with Manase and the medical porter in the rear. When

I could feel it coming, I found a boulder and threw up for the first time. Unfortunately, it wouldn't be the last. I began to realize I was getting weak. Ladi tried to calm me by walking with me at a *pole, pole* pace.

I was thirty minutes from the top of Mount Kilimanjaro—and from accomplishing one of my lifelong dreams—and I wasn't stopping now. I kept my head down and pushed onward and upward. I tried not to think about my stomach and how tired I was becoming.

Suddenly, the slope leveled out and there, in the not-so-far distance, probably fifty feet away, I saw it. It was the wooden, hand-painted sign that has become famous worldwide, the one marking Kili's summit. My adrenaline kicked in, and I started running with Martina. Ladi grabbed the camera and started videotaping us.

At 11:28 a.m. on October 7, 2018, after climbing more than 3,300 feet in about seven hours, we reached Kili's summit. I thanked Martina and hugged her. I hugged Ladi. I hugged Simon. I hugged Manase. Just being up there, with them, made me think about how amazing our God is. After battling so many medical problems as a child and teenager, I often wondered whether I would be able to do something so physically demanding. I felt so relieved, so happy. My sunglasses were fogging up from tears. I couldn't hold back my emotions.

"Simon, I'm so emotional. I'm crying. Thank you, thank you!"

"You're welcome," he told me. "This is why I do this. I love helping people reach their goals."

We gathered around the sign and took several photographs as a group. Then I took several photos of signs, including one for my Papi's upcoming nine-tieth birthday. We had been on Uhuru about fifteen minutes, and it was time to leave. It's not good for humans to be at that altitude for very long.

Besides, we still had to make our descent—and I had to throw up and use the bathroom again. I was so ready to get off the mountain. We had planned to do it in one day instead of the typical two or three days, but my body had other ideas.

We started by jogging down the mountain, seesawing through the rocks and sliding through scree. I'd have to stop, gag, and throw up, go to the restroom, and rest for a while. Then I'd feel better and start jogging again. It became a vicious roller coaster, in which I would feel okay and then not so great.

By then, because of my stomach bug and altitude sickness, Martina was convinced I was dehydrated. I couldn't keep liquids down. My oxygen level was only 86 percent, which isn't good. She knew I had to get off the mountain. She decided to stop giving me fluids because I just kept throwing up, which made me more dehydrated. We didn't bring an IV bag, which would have come in handy. When the antibiotics finally kicked in, I felt better and could eat something.

Rescues on Kili are never easy and are quite dangerous. We learned that firsthand when we encountered a woman who was lying on her side alone. She had fallen, only four hundred feet from the summit, and broken her leg and dislocated her shoulder. Her guide and the rest of her group had left her alone, promising to come back for her. Simon shook his head and decided to stay with her. He called the closest camp and told them about the situation. He would have to carry her down because a helicopter couldn't reach that altitude.

I was still woozy, and Martina advised Ladi that we were going to stop at Mweka Camp, at about 10,138 feet. It was only midday, and I was exhausted from the stomach pain, nausea, dehydration, and altitude sickness. I'd never felt so miserable—and I've obviously felt pretty bad before. Martina and I decided against a treatment, which would dehydrate me even more, and she gave me electrolytes. I slept through the night, throwing up now and then.

The next morning, I heard a helicopter flying overhead us in an attempt to rescue the injured woman. Ladi knocked on my tent and told me to get up. The porters brought us hot water to wash our dust-covered faces. I managed to eat two tiny bananas and part of an egg for breakfast.

That day, while descending the final 5,000 feet to Mweka Gate, I probably had to stop at least two dozen times to take care of business. Eventually, nothing was left in my system. I didn't have much strength and was wobbly, but I made it down on my own. I called my parents and told them I was down and safe.

We walked another mile to Simon's family farm. It was near the park border, and he fed us a wonderful meal of farm-fresh food. I managed to eat only a banana and a meat-filled pastry. There was a ceremony to say goodbye to the guides, cooks, and porters, and they sang and danced for us. Simon gave us a certificate confirming that we had reached Kili's summit.

After battling so many medical problems as a child and teenager, I often wondered whether I would be able to do something so physically demanding. I felt so relieved, so happy.

Now, about that Guinness World Record I mentioned. Almost a year after I reached Kili's summit, I submitted an application for the "Highest Elevation Enema Ever Performed." Two days before Christmas 2019, I received a response from Guinness. It read:

Dear JT Mestdah,

Thank you for sending us the details of your proposed record attempt for "Highest Elevation Enema Ever Performed."

Unfortunately, after thoroughly reviewing your application with members of our research team, we are afraid to say that we cannot accept your proposal as a Guinness World Records title.

Whilst we do not underestimate your proposal, we do not feel it would be appropriate to monitor this as a Guinness World Records title. Each and every application we receive is unique and has occurred as a result of different circumstances, however each record we verify must be standardisable and we do not feel that would be possible in this case.

Once again thank you for contacting Guinness World Records.

Kind regards,
Records Management Team

The letter also pointed me to the Guinness World Records website for details on "what makes a record." So I went there and here are the requirements for Guinness to recognize a world record:

- "Measurable—Can it be measured objectively?" My response: Yes, it is indeed measurable in actual feet in terms of elevation.

- "Breakable—Can the record be broken?" My response: Yes, it can most certainly be broken by anyone else who climbs Mount Kilimanjaro or any other of the world's tallest peaks—or perhaps even someone who might have to go on an airplane on a transatlantic flight.

- Standardisable—Can the record be repeated by someone else? Is it possible to create a set of parameters and conditions that all challengers can follow?" My response: According to published reports, there are about 750,000 people in the United States living with ostomy bags and more than 500,000 with some type of stoma. There are another 700,000 people in Europe who have had some type of ostomy surgery. The global market for ostomy drainage bags is expected to reach $4.1 billion by 2027.[233] Chances are that many of them, like me, need some type of treatment or enema.

- "Verifiable—Can the claim be proven? Will

there be accurate evidence available to prove it occurred?" My response: Yes, it's verifiable. There were at least ten other people with me when the record occurred, including Ladi, Martina, Simon, and Manase. There are also altitude coordinates from my GPS, which would verify exactly where I was when I established the world record.[234]

I'm also confident that my world record would meet the other requirements: "based on one variable," meaning the record is based on one superlative (an enema), and one unit of measurement (highest altitude in feet), and being "the best in the world" because the record for an enema at the highest elevation isn't currently in the *Guinness World Records* books, and my Google searches for any comparable feats have come up empty.[235] My record also can't be excluded for endangering or harming animals, excessive eating, food wastage, or the consumption of large amounts of alcohol in acts such as binge drinking or speed drinking.

As you can see, my record application meets all the criteria set by Guinness, and I'm dumbfounded as to why my record is not included in its latest edition of world records. I'm determined to get to the, uh, bottom of it!

Guinness says it also assesses all new records "against our values of integrity, respect, inclusiveness and passion."[236] It seems to me that a record that might inspire the other millions of people around the world who have dealt with health problems, specifically VATER and other ostomy conditions related to colorectal cancer, bladder cancer, Crohn's disease, or other gastro or bowel diseases, meets those criteria. It certainly would make the database of records more inclusive.

I know one thing for certain: I've tried to live my life with integrity, respect, inclusiveness, and passion, and hopefully I inspired other people to do the same by climbing Mount Kilimanjaro.

CHAPTER FOURTEEN

Learn and Don't Stop

....

THE GREAT AMERICAN investor Warren Buffett once estimated that he spends 80 percent of each day reading.[237] He starts every morning by reading his favorite newspapers like the *Wall Street Journal*, the *New York Times*, *USA Today*, and *Financial Times*.[238] Once Buffett gets to his office, he reads hundreds of pages of corporate reports and financial analysis. He estimates that he reads five hundred pages every day.

Buffett's goal is quite simple: to go to bed each night a little smarter.[239]

And it's hard to argue with the results. Buffett, known as the "Oracle of Omaha," is the sixth-wealthiest person in the world, according to *Forbes*, with an estimated net worth of $103.9 billion in August 2021.[240] His firm, Berkshire Hathaway, owns companies like Dairy Queen, GEICO, Fruit of the Loom, and Duracell. Buffett isn't perfect when it comes to investing, and I'm sure he has bought into a few lemons, but he has a higher batting average—and checking balance—than most because he read, did his homework, and made educated decisions.

In other words, Buffett, even at age ninety, has never stopped learning.

"Read 500 pages like this every day," he once said. "That's how knowledge works. It builds up, like compound interest. All of you can do it, but I guarantee not many of you will do it."[241]

Mr. Buffett is right. Most of us no longer have the time (or attention span) to read for three or four hours each day. We're too busy to stop and read a book, newspaper, or magazine in solitude. I guess that's why so many newspapers and magazines are going out of business. Our habits have changed.

But do you know how else we can continue to learn? By listening to others. Our friends, families, and strangers are a wealth of knowledge. If you took the time to have meaningful conversations with the people around you, you would be extremely surprised by what you'd learn from their experiences.

About a year ago, I launched a video interview and podcast series series called "JT Jester Speaks." I wanted to share meaningful stories and life lessons with my subscribers, and I also sought to continue to learn through my conversations with the subjects. And let me tell you: I can't believe what I have already learned!

The legendary UCLA basketball coach John Wooden, who guided the Bruins to ten NCAA national championships in a twelve-year span, often repeated the quote, "It's what you learn after you know it all that counts."[242]

Think about that statement. We should never stop learning. We've been learning from the day we were born. As babies, we learned how to walk and talk. When we were toddlers, we learned how to count and recite the alphabet. In high school, we learned subjects like geometry, calculus, chemistry, and geography. In so many ways, life is a never-ending lesson.

> *We should never stop learning. . . . life is a never-ending lesson.*

I know I've learned so much from the wonderful people I've interviewed, and their lessons have been invaluable to me. Here are some of my favorite episodes and the lessons I learned:

Be a "Let-It-Go-Er": I was fortunate enough to speak to author Steve Carter, a former teaching pastor at Willow Creek Community Church in Chicago. Steve has written three books: *The Best of You*, *This Invitational Life*, and *The Thing Beneath the Thing*.

More than anything, Steve is a wonderful communicator, storyteller, pastor, and teacher. He realizes how good stories can help teach us lessons from the Bible and bring Jesus into every conversation.

"I think stories are so impactful, right, because it's kind of this sense of the soul of an idea," Steve told me. "So I can transfer a thought. I can study, I can learn some facts, and I can transfer information. But it's so much different when I speak from a transformed place where that idea has taken up residence within my life. And it's taught me some things that I'm beginning then to see all around me."[243]

Steve shared with me a sweet story of how he was putting his daughter to bed one night while reading her the popular children's book *Chicka Chicka Boom Boom*. All of a sudden, Steve's daughter asked him, "Dad, do you want to know the most powerful word?"

"What is that?" he asked her.

"The most powerful word is *forgiveness* because you move from being a holder-on-er to a let-it-go-er."

Before Steve could tell his daughter how brilliant her statement was, she asked him, "Are you a holder-on-er or are you a let-it-go-er?"

"She took me to church at like nine fifteen at night," Steve told me. "See, I could talk about forgiveness, and all of a sudden I could tell all these amazing verses and facts, and then I can tell that story about my daughter. And then just say, 'Are any of you a holder-on-er? Any of you holding on to something that someone said or did?' It just makes it so much more accessible and applicable. And that's what Jesus was a master at."[244]

I agree so much with Steve. Painting the picture,

sharing a story or parable, or providing an illustration to a life lesson is so much more impactful than simply saying words or reading Scripture. The audience needs to see what you're saying to get a complete understanding of what you're trying to share.

His daughter's question got Steve thinking about forgiveness and what it means. He read Psalm 22, which includes the most anguished cry in human history: "My God, my God, why have you forsaken me?" (v. 1). Jesus cried out those words as He was suffering on the cross, after He offered Himself up for the sins of His people.

"It's powerful because He's not saying, 'God, why have you forsaken me,' which is often the human question," Steve said. "He's saying and quoting [David], who said, 'My God, why have you forsaken me?' So there's a personal connection and a real personal-like realization that both are true—*my* God and feeling a sense of forsaken or abandonment or neglect or forgotten. And I think that's part of a human existence. And so, you're gonna turn to something. You're gonna trust something in the midst of the desert. You're gonna trust something in the midst of a deserted place. And for me, that anchor is in Christ."[245]

I've thought about Steve's question many times in my life. When I've been wounded mentally or physically, whom do I lean on and where do I go for answers? I always go to Jesus Christ for answers because of my faith in the Lord. I've been blessed to have that relationship with Him to carry me through those difficult moments.

My relationship with Jesus is never more important than when I'm trying to forgive someone who might have wronged me. Steve has an interesting take on forgiveness too.

"Forgiveness is a solo sport," he said. "Forgiveness is . . . like *me*. I'm choosing not to be a holder-on-er. I'm choosing to release that at the cross. I'm choosing to send it away. . . . But reconciliation is different. Reconciliation now takes two people that now have to identify and come to a place of acceptance over what has transpired to create this wound."

That's where it can get a little complicated, according to Steve.

"Some people might say, 'I didn't do that,' or some people might not want to be at a place to acknowledge truth, or some people might not be ready to go on that path towards reconciliation," he told me. "And so that's, that's really, really tricky. And just because I've forgiven once doesn't mean I'm not gonna have to forgive tomorrow and the next day and the next day and the next day."[246]

How the other person reacts is equally important. Will they be a holder-on-er or a let-it-go-er?

"They're not thinking about what they said to you, but you're holding it still," Steve said. "Just 'cause you release that doesn't mean now you're totally back into great connection with that person. So that's the hard part: yes, the wound is releasing, forgiving, but then, too, praying towards an openness, a transparency, a repentance, an honesty about what this person did so that you can move forward together."[247]

Think about it: are you a holder-on-er or a let-it-go-er? Are you forgiving but not reconciling with those who have hurt you in the past? Sometimes, it's just so hard to forgive. What I've realized is that once I do have that moment of being able to forgive someone for doing something that I felt wronged me or hurt me, it allows me to move on. It also helps our relationship grow stronger, and I think that's so powerful.

Choose Your Attitude: Shortly after Nick Strand met Brianna Oas, she told him that doctors had diagnosed her with cystic fibrosis at age three. At

> *My relationship with Jesus is never more important than when I'm trying to forgive someone who might have wronged me.*

the time, doctors told her parents that she might not live to be thirteen.[248]

Cystic fibrosis, a genetic disorder, affects about thirty thousand people in the United States, according to the Cystic Fibrosis Foundation. The aggressive disease causes certain proteins to become dysfunctional, which causes mucus in various organs to become "thick and sticky."[249]

When Brianna was a toddler, she suffered from multiple ear infections, coughing, and a couple of bouts of pneumonia. Her parents took her to the Children's Hospital of Seattle, where doctors told them not to worry about the signs of cystic fibrosis and that her condition was probably only asthma. Tragically, she was among the rare few with CF.[250]

Brianna never let her condition affect the way she lived her life. She graduated from high school, attended Washington State University, and wanted to become a veterinarian.[251]

Brianna loved animals and tacos. After they married, she and Nick had two dogs, four cats, two horses, two cows, a tortoise, a hedgehog, and a potbellied pig.[252]

Nick and Brianna dated four years before they married in 2011. She was working as a veterinary technician; he was working as a videographer for Taylor Swift.[253]

They dealt with her medical struggles together, and he learned several important lessons along the way.

"Through her journey, she kind of was given a death sentence that a lot of us sometimes take for granted, as we don't have those struggles," Nick told me. "But she turned it into a quality. She turned it into a strength. And one of the big things that I found to love about her [was] she took this huge, heavy burden and was able to overcome it."

The most important thing Brianna taught Nick was this: "Choose your attitude, create your life."[254]

Tragically, Brianna died in 2017. She was twenty-eight. A few months before her death, she testified in front of Congress about the need for government funding for research into infectious organisms.[255] Only a few days before she died, she wrote a letter to her brother-in-law's brother, who was dying of ALS, and encouraged him not to be worried about getting a feeding tube. She was always thinking of others. She was always kind.[256]

Her father told the local newspaper in Washington that she had lived "60-something years in 20-something years. She was full of poise and grace, and her faith in Jesus Christ was so strong."[257]

Nick told me that he struggled mightily after Brianna's death. He wanted to write a book about their lives together, but he couldn't muster the strength or energy to put it on paper. That changed one morning when he woke up and couldn't feel the left side of his face.

"I was shocked. I thought it was a stroke," Nick said. "Come to find out it was simply Bell's palsy. But it was a great wake-up call. It reminded me that life is fragile. It reminded me that just overnight the feeling on the left side of your face could go away, which then also showed me that your lungs could stop, your heart could stop, your brain. And so that was my turn on. That was my, 'Okay, if not now, then when?' And so, I started writing."[258]

Nick ended up writing a beautiful book, *Love Someone Who Is Dying: Choose Your Attitude, Create Your Life!* The book details his relationship with Brianna and her fight against CF. The writing process was therapeutic for him. He learned to embrace his feelings, whether they were happy or sad, so he could process how to cope with her death.

"Instead of resisting, what I tried to do is, I tried to learn how to understand it, how to live within it, because then what that does is that gives us strength to be able to process those feelings as opposed to resist them," Nick said. "And so that's what helps us actually move along and helps us prepare."

Nick saw that lesson every day in his wife.

"For example, in the story with Brianna and her cystic fibrosis, instead of hiding it or pushing it away, she embraced it. She shared it. She became vulnerable on that as a way to test herself and to help create herself and build that character. So, you know, that's what I would say is less resisting and more trying to understand and be okay to feel—whether it's sad [or] happy."[259]

Nick's book allowed him to create a "Choose Your Attitude" lifestyle brand to honor his wife.[260]

Through his work, Nick is helping others cope with loving someone who is dying while also helping them live life to the fullest. He's an author, speaker, life coach, and entrepreneur, and he continues to work as a videographer and LED technician for acts such as Kelly Clarkson, Maroon 5, and the Dave Matthews Band. Now, that's living life to the fullest!

Most importantly, Nick is hoping to one day fulfill his wife's wish of making CF stand for "Cure Found."[261]

There's no question we have all been through trials and tribulations at times. They help us keep things in perspective and help us live our lives to the fullest. I love how Nick and Brianna put such a positive spin on something so tragic and how they lived each day loving each other and Christ. It's an empowering message. We all want to bring positivity to the world and encourage and lift up others.

God Will Meet You: Daniel Foy grew up not far from me in Grosse Pointe, Michigan. He was born only eleven days before me, on September 2, 1995, and also faced serious health complications from birth.

Just before doctors and nurses were about to send Daniel home with his family, they discovered that he had a rare heart condition called hypoplastic left heart syndrome, which is diagnosed when the left side of the heart is underdeveloped. The Centers for Disease Control and Prevention (CDC) estimates that about "1 out of every 3,841 babies born in the United States each year is born with hypoplastic left heart syndrome."[262]

"In my case, it was so underdeveloped to the point where I basically didn't have the left side; I was basically . . . born with only the right side of my heart," Daniel told me, adding that he had "only half of [a] heart."[263]

If you've ever met Daniel, you would know that statement couldn't be further from the truth.

Surgeons presented Daniel's parents with three options: a heart transplant, which was unheard of for a newborn a quarter century ago and probably wouldn't be successful; taking him home so that he might survive for a couple of weeks; or putting Daniel through three open-heart surgeries over the course of about eighteen months to try to correct his cardiac problems.

"[The surgeries] would fix the congenital heart defect," Daniel said. "But, you know, there's no guarantees, but it's the safest way and the best bet. So my parents decided on doing that."[264]

Daniel had his first open-heart surgery when he was only four days old. He had another one when he was just six months old and a third when he was eighteen months old. There were severe complications with the third surgery.

"That surgery, unfortunately, went horribly wrong," he said. "I don't know what went wrong, but after the surgery, I was diagnosed with a very, very rare lung condition."[265]

That lung condition is called plastic bronchitis. According to Penn Medicine, plastic bronchitis "is a condition where buildup in your airways forms into casts that look similar to tree branches. The casts are made of mucus and cellular materials and have a soft, rubbery consistency. You might cough them up as your lungs try to clear the airways."[266]

Daniel described the casts as cotton balls with tails. He coughed up casts as large as his dad's thumb. At age two, he went into hospice care but fought with everything he had and survived.[267] Two years later, he was airlifted to the hospital during a Florida beach vacation when the condition returned. He survived again.

One of the things Daniel missed most while growing up as a kid was playing sports. He was able to play soccer until he was about seven. He loved watching University of Michigan football games more than anything.[268]

Daniel's first three heart surgeries were at the C.S. Mott Children's Hospital at the University of Michigan. But even after those multiple surgeries with highly skilled doctors, Daniel's heart condition worsened. Eventually, his doctors realized that he might not live much longer without a heart transplant. Doctors put his name on a transplant list, and he and his family anxiously waited for a donor.

It was during this difficult time that Daniel leaned on God quite a bit. One day, while Daniel was lying on the couch, he had an epiphany.

"I had like a coughing fit," he said. "God didn't, like, speak to me, and I didn't have the Bible open, but I kind of just remember this . . . parable, where it said, 'When you are at your lowest, God will meet you there.'"

It was the exact encouragement Daniel needed to hear. God *was* speaking to him.

"Yeah, I'm at a very low point. I'm super sick," he said. "I don't know if I can make it to high school."[269]

One day shortly thereafter, Daniel was shooting baskets at a friend's house. His friend's father rushed out of the house, scooped up Daniel, and placed him inside his BMW. Then he drove as fast as possible to Daniel's house. His parents and a couple of close family friends were waiting on the front porch. Doctors had found him a new heart.

On July 22, 2013, the next morning, Daniel had his fourth open-heart surgery. During the fourteen-hour surgery, he suffered a massive stroke on the right side of his brain. Doctors completed the delicate surgery and placed him in a medically induced coma for two-and-a-half weeks. When Daniel woke up, he was blind in his left eye and partially blind in his right.[270] He still has only partial use of his left arm and left hand.

Despite these obstacles, Daniel fought through rehabilitation and finished high school. He attended the aptly named Hope College in Holland, Michigan, where he majored in communications. He continued to fulfill his love of sports by working as a manager on the football team.[271]

That's probably the most important lesson that I've learned from my friendship with Daniel. When faced with obstacles and hardships, many of us might evaluate our circumstances as having a life that is half-empty. Because of medical problems, maybe we can't play sports or do physical activities like other kids. Because of learning differences, maybe we can't read or write like everyone else.

Daniel took the exact opposite approach. Even though he couldn't play football or run track, he embraced his love of sports. He learned to kayak and continued to participate in sports in other ways.

Like Daniel, I was confident that Jesus would meet me when I was at the lowest point of my medical and educational difficulties. No matter what we're facing in life, we know in our hearts that Jesus will not allow us to go through it alone. When it feels like the bottom has given way, and we've fallen into darkness, God will let us know He is there. Daniel and I can certainly attest to that.

Let God Use You: Aaron Boyd grew up in East Belfast, Northern Ireland. He admits that he went to church when he was younger only to make his parents happy. It wasn't until he was a teenager that he truly accepted Jesus into his life; he did that on the side of a road.[272]

"My two friends were there, and I was just like, 'I need to give my life to the Lord,'" Aaron told me. "And I just gave my life to the Lord that night, and that was it. No turning back, just went for it."[273]

Eventually, Aaron became a spiritual leader and was heavily involved in youth worship in Belfast. He helped found the contemporary Christian band Bluetree out of Belfast's Christian Fellowship Church in 2004.[274]

Shortly thereafter, one of Aaron's pastors asked him to join a group on a mission trip to Thailand. Aaron and his bandmates played at a couple of churches and a twenty-four-hour worship service. Near the end of the two-week mission trip, Aaron asked one of the pastors if there was anywhere else they could play.

That night, they ended up performing in the most unlikely of destinations—inside the Climax Bar in the red-light district of Walking Street in Pattaya,

Thailand.[275] According to a UNAIDS report, Thailand has more than 120,000 sex workers, including at least 40 percent under the age of eighteen.[276] Police say there are more than 100,000 arrests involving human trafficking in Thailand each year, and about 90 percent of the child abuse cases involve foreigners.[277]

Pattaya is a popular coastal destination for foreigners, and authorities consider the city's red-light district to be one of the worst sex trafficking hotspots in the world.

"The entire fabric and DNA and culture of that seaside town is prostitution, exploitation, modern-day slavery," Aaron said. "It exists, and I'd never seen that before. The place is broken up into different *sois*, and that's just a different district, so if you want one thing, you go here. If you want transgender, you go here. If you want male homosexual, you go here, if you want whatever. There's just different areas. . . . I'd never seen guys with menus selling certain things. . . . And I was like, 'This is weird, and wrong, just flat-out wrong.'"[278]

One of the best things about not speaking the native language in a place like Thailand is that so much gets lost in translation. Aaron figures that's the only way the Thai bar owner agreed to let a Northern Irish Christian band play in the joint, which had a brothel upstairs. "The bar owner didn't understand exactly who we were," Aaron said. "I think all she knew is there was an Irish band that was gonna play for free and they had a strong fan base."[279]

He hoped they could play for two hours. He describes what happened next as being prophetic or perhaps even the result of divine intervention.

"Call it whatever you want," Aaron said. "I just started to sing, 'You're the God of this city, King of these people, greater things have yet to come.' And basically sang that song. . . . I had all these lines just written down, and afterwards didn't really think much of it, just jotted all this stuff down."[280]

Throughout the mission trip, Aaron and his roommate had been dialoguing and processing everything they were seeing and experiencing in Thailand.

"You start to ask all these questions, and that's ultimately where this song came from," Aaron said. "We'd be having these conversations, and we'd be like, 'Where is God in the middle of all of this? Like, whose responsibility is that? What the heck is going on here? And then, you know, they hold the king in such high esteem [in Thailand]. And we're like, 'What kind of king lets this go on in their kingdom?'"[281]

Aaron and his bandmates returned to Belfast and continued singing at a monthly event where they led worship. They added an introduction, bridge, and ending to the song that became known as "God of This City." Bluetree recorded the track on their 2007 album, *Greater Things*.

No matter what we're facing in life,
we know in our hearts that
Jesus will not allow us to go through
it alone. When it feels
like the bottom has given way,
and we've fallen into darkness,
God will let us know He is there.

Shortly thereafter, Bluetree opened for American worship singer Chris Tomlin during a worship conference in Belfast. Tomlin heard "God of This City" and was blown away.[282]

"It just caught me," Tomlin said of the song. "[I] just went, 'Wow, what is that?' . . . We were going to do these cities around the country and going to these different cities, Dallas, Boston, L.A., Chicago, some of the major cities of the US, and I knew this would be a great song to sing over these cities. Then a world tour was going to be coming up, and I knew singing over these cities in the world would be amazing."[283]

Tomlin asked Bluetree if he could record their

song and play it around the world, and they happily agreed. "God of This City" became an anthem for Passion Conferences, churches, and other worship events around the world.

"That was the start of doors just beginning to open," Aaron said. "But honestly at that moment, when the doors began to open, my family, we made the commitment, and with a couple other friends as well, it was like anything that we do in our lives, we want to help people meet Jesus, and we want to help a bunch of kids across the world who do not have a voice. And in everything, that's the thread that goes through."[284]

Over the years, Aaron has sung over girls rescued from sex trafficking in Cambodia, encouraged church leaders in Myanmar, and played concerts and helped orphans and vulnerable children in Haiti, Guatemala, South Africa, and other parts of the world.[285]

It's wonderful that Aaron is allowing God to use him in many ways. Remember that God isn't worried about what we don't have. He is only interested in what we have that can help Him bring people to Jesus. How are you letting God use your talents and skills? What can you do to help and bless others? Let go, let Jesus into your heart, and allow Him to use you to influence change in the world like Aaron.

Make God Famous: YoungMin You was born in Seoul, South Korea, as a pastor's kid. His father was a church planter and pastor, and YoungMin and his family moved quite a bit. They didn't have much money. In fact, at one point, he and his mother, father, and sister were living in a fifty-square-foot apartment—without indoor plumbing.

"To give you a perspective, fifty square feet is about like the size of an average American bathroom," YoungMin told me. "So in this room . . . the four of us would lay down together, and that would be our bed, a sheet or blanket across the room. And we'd literally lay down together and sleep together there. So it was a tiny room and we didn't even have a bathroom."[286]

When YoungMin's parents couldn't pay the rent for that apartment, they moved in with his grandmother. Her apartment wasn't much bigger than the previous one, and she was caring for YoungMin's disabled uncle. Then his younger sister was born, so the eight of them were crammed into the tiny space.[287] In South Korea, families mean everything, and their tight relationships and bonds are why many extended families choose to live together, but that doesn't mean the circumstances are easy.

Shortly after YoungMin's family moved back into their own place, his uncle committed suicide. It sent YoungMin into a tailspin.

"That was really, really difficult for me because I was living with him, and I saw his agony and struggles daily that he was going through," YoungMin said. "And I felt like I should have and could have done a better job at helping him and to share the gospel and just help him to get out of that rut. And I felt like I failed as his nephew. That had a huge impact on me."[288]

Because YoungMin's family moved so much, he changed schools frequently. Other students often bullied him because he was the new kid. To help him fit in, YoungMin joined a gang when he was thirteen.

"I became one of the gang members," he said. "I joined the group to protect myself, and we were doing some horrible things."[289]

YoungMin said his friends were affiliated with the mafia and were asked to do the overlords' dirty work.

"I felt really sad about my life," he said. "And there were times that I just felt really down and depressed. And I wanted some sort of like a change in my life. I felt extremely guilty and frustrated whenever I'd come back home. I remember just feeling miserable because at church . . . I was a perfect pastor's kid. People were like, 'Oh, YoungMin wouldn't do anything wrong.' But at that school, I was living the opposite life. I was a totally different person, just miserable and violent. And I'm like praying that something will change."[290]

God answered those prayers when YoungMin was offered a chance to attend school in the United States to learn English when he was fifteen.

"My parents, they are extremely loving and

gracious," YoungMin said. "They squeezed every-thing out financially to make me come to the States to study and allow me to pursue my dream."[291]

Being so far from home, YoungMin was often lonely and homesick. He didn't yet know English and missed Korean food. He bounced between several host families.

At his lowest point, YoungMin found happi-ness in his relationship with God and his love for music. His older sister had taken piano lessons, and YoungMin thought it was cool but his parents couldn't afford to send him to lessons too.

One of his host families had an upright piano in their home. He taught himself how to play by watching YouTube videos.[292]

"I realized there were two things that did not change on me from South Korea to the States," YoungMin said. "It was God and music for me. They stayed the same. And it was mind-boggling for me, I'm like, 'God, that I knew in Korea, was the same God here.' That's when I developed my personal relationship with God. That's when I got up in the morning and started saying hi to God and talked to Him and started my walk with Jesus."[293]

YoungMin became more committed to God and his music. Eventually, he realized his music made other people happy as well. By watching YouTube videos, he became an excellent pianist and composer.[294] "That's when I realized, 'Ooh, this is maybe my calling,' " he said. "I'm gonna pursue music more seriously, and that's what I felt like God was telling me."[295]

Despite his lack of professional training, his English had dramatically improved. He applied for admission to the Wheaton College Conservatory of Music in Wheaton, Illinois, to study composition.[296] If he didn't get accepted, he figured he would return to South Korea.

Even though other applicants had more experience, YoungMin was admitted. He was first in his class during his first semester, thanks to his hard work and his professors' patience and dedication.[297] And it paid off; today, he is able to pursue his passion and goal in life, which he says is "to make God famous through music."[298]

YoungMin has certainly done that. He met his wife, Chantelle, a vocal performance artist, at Wheaton College. They married in 2016 and settled in Michigan.[299]

In 2019, YoungMin released his debut album, *Walk on Water*. He is one of the most popular Christian composers on YouTube. His music videos have been viewed more than 5.5 million times.[300]

YoungMin is the perfect example of what can happen when you talk to God and truly listen. Through daily prayer, YoungMin realized that God wanted him to dedicate his life to music and compose songs that would help spread His name.

What can you do to spread the gospel? Mark 16:15–16 tells us, "Go into all the world and preach the gospel to all creation. Whoever believes and is baptized will be saved, but whoever does not believe will be condemned."

Hopefully, through my writing, podcasts, and foundation, I'm fulfilling God's wishes. Won't you join Pastor Steve, Nick, Daniel, Aaron, YoungMin, and me in helping spread the Word?

Never stop learning because life never stops teaching. Read each day. Listen to others. Make learning a habit and practice. Make sure it is part of your life every day. Take the time to invest in yourself. It's the most valuable thing you can do.

CHAPTER FIFTEEN

Leave a Legacy

....

IF YOU GREW UP in Detroit, the Motor City, you
probably have a deep love of automobiles. My dad
and I love cars, especially fast ones. We enjoy all cars,
especially the ones made right here in Detroit with
American blood, sweat, and tears.

Unless you grew up in the 1940s and 1950s
like my grandparents did, you might not know that
Detroit is famous for something else. After the United
States agreed to join the Allies to defeat Nazi Germany
and the Axis powers in World War II, the Motor City
became the center of America's military production.

Instead of building Fords, Chryslers, and
Chevrolets, Detroit's auto factory workers produced
tanks, munitions, airplanes, radar units, jeeps, amphib-
ious vehicles, and bullets. Detroit, with only 2 percent
of the country's population, was responsible for 10
percent of America's war production.[301]

Those efforts started in 1940, when United States
President Franklin Delano Roosevelt ordered General
Motors president William Knudsen to take charge of
the country's military production. At the New York
Auto Show later that year, Knudsen delivered the
keynote speech in which he told his fellow Motor City

executives, "Gentlemen, we must out-build Hitler."[302]

Believe it or not, this period of rapid expansion and automation in Detroit had a profound effect on my family's history. Before I share with you how that happened, I first have to tell you the amazing story of my maternal grandparents.

My grandfather, John Boll, was the son of Dutch immigrants. His mother and father came to the United States shortly after they married and didn't know a word of English. They settled in Detroit, where my grandfather was born in 1929. After high school, Papi, as we call him, joined the United States Army in 1951, six years after the Allies had defeated the Nazis.

While Papi was stationed at Fort Bragg, he and his buddies were in Raleigh, North Carolina, on a weekend pass. Just before they reached the base, they spotted three women hitchhiking on the side of the road. Papi dropped his buddies off, circled back around the block, and picked up the young women.

It turned out that the young ladies were members of the Roxy Theatre chorus line, or the Roxyettes, a famous line of precision dancers from a theatre located just off Times Square in New York. They were performing at the North Carolina State Fair and had missed their ride to the fairgrounds. To thank Papi for his kind gesture, the women said they would leave tickets for him at the gate.

That night, Papi and his buddies attended the

show, and Papi waved a white handkerchief from his seat to let one of the girls know he was there. That woman was my grandmother, Marlene Boll. Papi and his friends ended up taking Nani, as we call her, and her friends out to dinner that night.

To impress the girls, Papi and his friends told them that they were medical students from Columbia, South Carolina. That wasn't exactly true; Papi and his buddies were actually medics in the army. Over the next several months, Papi and Nani kept in touch through letters, and so did Papi's buddies and one of the other dancers. It was quite a chore for Papi and his friends to keep their stories straight.

Nani, who grew up in New Jersey, had been dancing since she was five years old. The Roxyettes performed on *The Ed Sullivan Show*, and soon thereafter she was invited to audition for the Radio City Rockettes. She danced with the legendary Rockettes from 1952 to 1954. Radio City Music Hall in New York became her home away from home. She high kicked in as many as five shows a day, seven days a week, for three weeks straight and then would have a week off.

After Papi left the army, he wanted to ask Nani to move back to Detroit with him. First, he had a confession to make. He drove to her mother's home in New Jersey and knocked on the front door. When Nani answered, he said, "I haven't been truthful to you. I'm not studying to be a doctor. I was a medic in the army." He handed her a scrapbook in which he'd explained everything.

"I'm staying at a motel down the road," he told her. "I'll be there for a couple of days. I want to marry you and want you to come to Detroit. If you can't do it and won't forgive me, I'll understand."

Fortunately for Papi, Nani agreed to go with him on one condition—that her mother, whom Nani was supporting financially, go to Detroit with them as well. Nani and Papi married on June 19, 1954.

Now, here's where we get back to Detroit. In the first two decades of the twentieth century, millions of Black Americans moved from the rural South to large cities in the Northeast, Midwest, and West in what historians call the Great Migration.[303] Then, another 4.3 million Black Americans left the South between 1940 to 1970, an exodus referred to as the Second Great Migration.

"African Americans went north to escape Jim Crow. They also sought better job opportunities. In the North, people were needed to work in factories during and after World War II. These jobs offered better wages and working conditions than were available in the South. . . . People from Arkansas and Alabama took the Illinois Central Railroad to Cleveland, Ohio; Chicago, Illinois; and Detroit, Michigan."[304]

When Ford began producing B-24 Liberator

bombers at a rate of one per hour outside Detroit, it needed tens of thousands of workers on its assembly lines. "The social landscape of the city changed greatly during the war. Within the first year and a half following the attack on Pearl Harbor, 350,000 workers from the American south and elsewhere moved to Detroit to join in the war effort. With holes in the labor force created by men entering military service, women were hired for factory labor, shifting norms and creating the folk hero 'Rosie the Riveter.'"[305]

It wasn't only Black citizens who moved to Detroit during this time. People came from all over the country came for the higher-paying jobs while others felt a sense of duty and patriotism to help America's war effort.

There was one big problem: the new workers who came to Detroit didn't have anywhere to live. At first, the Ford workers who relocated from other plants lived in government-built temporary dormitories. Others lived in garages, trailers, tent encampments, or shanties made of tin, wood, or any other material they could find. Even after World War II ended, there was a shortage of affordable housing for veterans who returned to Detroit and for blue-collar workers in the auto plants and other production facilities.[306]

That's where Papi came in. Neither Papi nor Nani attended college because their parents could not afford the tuition. They made up for their lack of formal education with hard work, dedication, and ingenuity. Papi's construction company literally started with a wheelbarrow and shovel—that's it. He did odd jobs around town in Roseville, Michigan, and Nani ran a dance studio out of the basement of their home to help make ends meet.

A couple of years later, Papi partnered with someone to start an excavating business, and Nani worked as their bookkeeper. In 1957, Papi founded Lakeview Construction Company, and in 1964, he decided to do something about the affordable housing shortage in Detroit. He founded Chateau Estates, a developer of manufactured home communities. Eventually his properties housed twenty thousand families throughout the Midwest and Florida. In 1993, Papi began selling Chateau Properties, Inc., a real estate investment trust, on the New York Stock Exchange at twenty dollars a share. Four years later, Chateau Properties, Inc. merged with Roc Communities of Colorado to become the largest developer of manufactured home communities in the United States.[307]

When Papi and the board agreed to sell the company to the Washington Pension Fund in 2003, the multibillion-dollar conglomerate's stock was worth $29.25 a share. By then, Chateau Properties, Inc.'s portfolio consisted of 229 communities in thirty-six states with a total of about one hundred thousand

Neither Papi nor Nani attended college because their parents could not afford the tuition. They made up for their lack of formal education with hard work, dedication, and ingenuity.

residential home sites. Papi says they were five-star properties, with clubhouses, swimming pools, and recreational areas. Residents were proud to live there.

As a way to give back to the community, Nani and Papi established the John A. and Marlene L. Boll Foundation in 1985. Over the last thirty-five years, the foundation has pledged more than $50 million in support of the arts, education, and health services in Michigan, around the United States, and across the world. My grandparents are so grateful for the way God has blessed our family, and they want to be faithful stewards to the resources entrusted in their care.

As the foundation's website says:

John and Marlene Boll have experienced great blessing and success through their business ventures and lifelong stewardship and investment practices. With gratitude and humility they have always sought to give back to the communities of which they have been a part by supporting education, the arts, and health services. John and Marlene have provided opportunities to those who have not experienced the advantages afforded to them, and have reached out with generosity and love in response to their own overwhelming sense of gratitude to God for His provision.

John and Marlene are a study in contrasts; he a rugged construction worker, as comfortable on a bulldozer as in a boardroom, and she a graceful and elegant dancer by profession, schooled in and appreciative of culture and the arts. Together the Bolls have created a legacy that envelops hard work, pragmatic and honest business practices, beauty, grace, concern for the poor, children, and those who deserve a break, acknowledgement of their faith in a Creator God, and a desire to improve the quality of life for the communities that they love.[308]

Over the years, Nani and Papi have given gener-
ously to hospitals, Christian-based organizations, the
arts, and other nonprofit groups. They've not only
given money through their foundation but have also
served on boards to raise funding for new construction projects that have served at-risk inner-city youth
and helped establish better schools for them in
Detroit. What a wonderful legacy!

What will your legacy be? How will others
remember you and your life after you are gone? Our
legacies are passed from one generation to the next,
and in many cases, they are all we leave behind. How
we live our lives and the actions we take each day
are how people will remember us. Whether at work,
school, church, or home, how we treat others and
how we act around them will shape our legacies.

Fortunately, there is still time to build your
legacy. If you don't have the financial resources to
be charitable, give your time, God-given talents,
and emotional support to those in need. Think
about how you treat others at work or school. Smile
and greet your fellow students or employees, offer
them compliments, and encourage them whenever
you can. Mentor younger employees at work, or, if
you're an older student in school, take a freshman or
sophomore under your wings, show them the ropes,
and look out for them. Most importantly, act like
someone others will want to look up to—be nice!

Live the way you want others to remember you.

And, of course, always be kind.

* * *

When you have faced as many health obstacles as me, you think about your life and legacy often. Hopefully, I've made a positive impact on my family, friends, schools, and communities with my faith, attitude, empathy, and spirit. I sure hope I have had a positive effect on the people I love. I know I have worked hard to be that kind of person.

Just a couple of years ago, I decided to follow in my grandparents' footsteps and establish the JT Mestdagh Foundation. My hope is that by "reaching up and reaching out, the JT Mestdagh Foundation [will see] a world changed and improved by children with congenital colorectal issues who receive world-class medical care, and by those with dyslexia and other learning differences who excel with the best possible educational testing, mentoring, and tutoring, especially using the Tattum Reading program." My foundation also "envisions these young people's families, caregivers, and educators surrounded with love and hope as well as practical tools and creative strategies to ease the demands that no one should face alone."[309]

When I was growing up, my parents and I faced those same obstacles and challenges alone because the proper testing, mentoring, and tutoring wasn't in place. I didn't know how to read—and feared that I would never learn how—until God intervened. I was blessed to meet Steve Tattum, who changed my life forever. My parents and I remain steadfastly committed to bringing the Tattum Reading program to the Grosse Pointe Public School System, as well as other school districts around Michigan to help students with learning differences.

I'm also excited that Steve is working with Beyond Basics, a student- and family-centered, literacy-focused nonprofit organization in Detroit. Beyond Basics has been around since 1999, and its president, Pamela Good, started working with Steve a few years later to better serve its students. Beyond Basics says it consistently helps students achieve grade-level reading in six weeks with one-on-one tutors under Steve's program.[310] In 2018, Detroit Public Schools had the lowest standardized test scores in the country with 95 percent of fourth graders not being proficient in reading and 93 percent not being proficient in math.[311] There are so many students there who need our help.

Live the way you want others to remember you.

Today, Beyond Basics has more than 1,500 volunteers and 107 staff members who are helping thousands of students in metropolitan Detroit schools learn to read and write.[312] In October 2018, with the help of General Motors,[313] Beyond Basics opened the doors to the Beyond Basics Family Literacy Center, which helps teach families to read and provides help with GED and SAT preparation, essay writing support, and workplace development programs.[314] Pamela and her staff are doing great work.

Hopefully, with my work in helping children and adults learn to read and write, and the work I'm doing to help children with VATER syndrome and other congenital colorectal issues, I'll leave a legacy that my children and grandchildren will one day be proud of. I know one thing for certain: I couldn't be prouder of my grandparents. I'm working hard every day to be remembered as they one day will be. I'm trying to be kind, considerate, and generous.

Shortly before longtime *Jeopardy* host Alex Trebek died in November 2020, ABC News reporter Michael Strahan asked him how he would want to be remembered. Over thirty-seven years, millions of TV viewers around the world welcomed Trebek into their homes as the host of the popular trivia game. He replaced Bob Barker, the longtime host of *The Price Is Right*, as the *Guinness World Records* holder for hosting the most game show episodes.[315]

In March 2019, Trebek announced to the world that doctors had diagnosed him with stage 4 pancreatic cancer.[316] Over his final months, he was showered with love and support.

"What you see on air, really, is what I am," Trebek told Strahan. "I'm a reasonably nice guy, and I'd like you to view me that way. I don't go out of my way to malign anybody. I want to be considered as helpful and generous and kind. You know, enjoy life, and make somebody laugh. I believe laughter is one of the greatest cures that we can have. It's right up there with prayer, believe me."[317]

He said, "I've had such a good life. There is no possibility of any regrets in my mind or in my heart, so I'm happy."[318]

Can't we all be so lucky?

As I begin the second quarter of my life, God is still throwing me curveballs. He must think there's a hole in my swing! I'm still dealing with the symptoms of VATER, or VACTERAL syndrome, as doctors commonly refer to it now. This mostly means continuing to manage my bowel control and bone abnormalities, which add to my discomfort.

Doctors also diagnosed me with having Klippel Feil syndrome (KFS), which is a rare condition that affects the development of the bones in my spine. According to the National Institutes of Health, people with KFS are born with "abnormal fusion of

I'm going to keep a smile on my face and try to make the people around me happy because there are no bad days. . . . only hard days.

at least two spinal bones (vertebrae) in the neck. Common features may include a short neck, low hairline at the back of the head, and restricted movement of the upper spine. Some people with KFS have no symptoms. Others may have frequent headaches, back and neck pain, and other nerve issues. People with KFS are at risk for severe spinal injury." The NIH estimates that one in 40,000 people have KFS.[319] Wouldn't you know it? I'm one of them.

It's getting more difficult for me to turn my head without discomfort, like when I'm looking both ways while driving, and my neck is sometimes stiff and sore. I crack my neck to make it better.

And, finally, I have a tethered spinal cord for the third time in my life. Fortunately, for me, I have stopped growing, so my spinal cord isn't under too much tension. My back sometimes gets stiff, and I sometimes feel a tingling or electric-like current from my thigh to my heel. For the most part, as long as I keep moving, stretching, and exercising, I can manage the problem pretty well.

I know one thing: I'm going to keep a smile on my face and try to make the people around me happy because there are no bad days. . . . only hard days.

Acknowledgments

THANK YOU to my Lord and Savior, Jesus Christ, who has healed me so many times and has given me the strength and courage to get up again. I know I wouldn't be where I am today without my steadfast faith.

Thank you to my parents, Jim and Kristine Mestdagh, who stood up for me when I wasn't old enough or strong enough to do it myself, and for teaching me never to let my differences or any obstacle stand in the way of accomplishing everything God has envisioned for me.

Thank you to my grandparents, Papi and Nani and Pa and Ma, for loving me, encouraging me, and supporting me throughout my life.

Thank you to my mentors, friends, doctors, tutors, and teachers, so many of whom are named in this book. Without your friendship, guidance, patience, and kindness, none of this would have been possible.

Thank you so much to Anita Palmer, Jenn David, Greg Lucid, and the team at Forefront Books for believing in me and allowing me to share my story of encouragement. I hope it changes a few lives along the way.

A tremendous thank-you to Mark Schlabach for putting my thoughts and words into a story that I pray touches lives!

Notes

1. Society for Neuroscience, "Dyslexia: What Brain Research Reveals About Reading," LD Online, 2004, http://www.ldonline.org/article/10784/.

2. Lauren Melnick, "Mount Kilimanjaro Facts: What You Need to Know About Africa's Highest Peak," GVI, 2019, https://www.gviusa.com/blog/mount-kilimanjaro-facts-what-you-need-to-know-about-africas-highest-peak/.

3. "Is Climbing Kilimanjaro Safe?," Ultimate Kilimanjaro, accessed August 13, 2021, https://www.gviusa.com/blog/mount-kilimanjaro-facts-what-you-need-to-know-about-africas-highest-peak/.

4. Alex Dixon, "Kindness Makes You Happy . . . and Happiness Makes You Kind," *Greater Good*, University of California Berkeley, September 6, 2011, https://greatergood.berkeley.edu/article/item/kindness_makes_you_happy_and_happiness_makes_you_kind.

5. "Imperforate Anus," University of California San Francisco Benioff Children's Hospitals, accessed August 13, 2021, https://www.ucsfbenioffchildrens.org/conditions/imperforate-anus.

6. "Pediatric VATER Syndrome (VACTERL Association)," Children's Health, accessed August 15, 2021, https://www.childrens.com/specialties-services/conditions/vater-syndrome-vacterl-association.

7. Emily Perl Kingsley, "Welcome to Holland," 1987. Reprinted with the author's permission.

8. "What is Down Syndrome?" National Down Syndrome Society, accessed July 16, 2020, https://www.ndss.org/about-down-syndrome/down-syndrome/.

9. Dawn Alsept, "Welcome to Holland—Interview with Author Emily Perl Kingsley," Cedar's Story, November 4, 2019, https://www.cedarsstory.com/welcome-holland-interview-author-emily-perl-kingsley/.

10. Mary H. J. Farrell, "Growing Up Down," *People*, May 2, 1994, https://people.com/archive/growing-up-down-vol-41-no-16/.

11. Farrell.

12. Alsept, "Welcome to Holland—Interview with Author Emily Perl Kingsley."

13. Jason Kingsley and Mitchell Levitz, *Count Us In: Growing Up with Down Syndrome* (1994; repr., Orlando: Harvest, 2007), 25.

14. Jill Lepore, "How We Got to Sesame Street," *New Yorker*, May 11, 2020, https://www.newyorker.com/magazine/2020/05/11/how-we-got-to-sesame-street.

15. Kingsley and Levitz, viii.

16. "About Me" page on Emily Perl Kingsley's website, accessed August 13, 2021, https://www.emilyperlkingsley.com/emily-history.

17. Kingsley and Levitz, 183.

18. "About Me."

19. Farrell, "Growing Up Down."

20. Alsept, "Welcome to Holland: Interview with Author Emily Perl Kingsley."

21. "Who We Are," *Our Daily Bread* (website), accessed August 13, 2021, https://odb.org/who-we-are.

22. "Timeline of Major Events," *Our Daily Bread* (website), accessed August 13, 2021, https://odb.org/our-story.

23. Dave Branon, "Trust Him with Your Heart," *Our Daily Bread*, September 13, 1995, https://odb.org/US/1995/09/13/trust-him-with-your-heart.

24. Bowie Kuhn, *Hardball* (1987; repr., Lincoln, NB: University of Nebraska Press, 1997), 298.

25. Pat Williams, "Watson Spoelstra," in *It's Not Who You Know, It's Who You Are: Life Lessons from Winners* (Grand Rapids, MI: Revell, 2015).

26. Watson Spoelstra, "Joe Louis Trains for Simon Bout in Down-Town Ballroom," *Eugene Register-Guard*, March 13, 1941, https://news.google.com/newspapers?id=r-KARAAAAIBAJ&sjid=l-gDAAAAIBAJ&dq=spoelstra&pg=3450%2C2727275; Watson Spoelstra, "He Still Can Run!," *Youngstown Vindicator*, March 8, 1944, https://news.google.com/newspapers?id=1YxIAAAAIBAJ&sjid=o4MMAAAAI-BAJ&dq=spoelstra&pg=4095%2C1921463.

27. "Miami Heat Q&A: What Would Erik Spoelstra Write About His Team If He Followed His Grandfather's Footsteps," *Palm Beach Post*, December 29, 2016, https://www.palmbeachpost.com/2016/12/29/miami-heat-q-a-what-would-erik-spoelstra-write-about-his-team-if-he-followed-in-his-grandfathers-footsteps/.

28. Kuhn, *Hardball*, 298–99.

29. "Media Information," *Baseball Chapel*, accessed August 13, 2021, http://baseballchapel.org/index.cfm?Fuseaction=MediaInformation&C-FID=17868538&CFTOKEN=bbfb11c4a664b3b4-BC1300B7-A7AE-A9E0-E3F261328663250E.

30. *Baseball Chapel* (website), accessed August 13, 2021, http://www.baseballchapel.org/.

31. "Watson Spoelstra," New Netherland Institute, accessed August 13, 2021, https://www.newnetherlandinstitute.org/history-and-heritage/dutch_americans/watson-spoelstra/.

32. "Erik Spoelstra," *NBA* (website), accessed August 13, 2021, https://www.nba.com/heat/contact/directoryspoelstrahtml.

33. Debbie Donovan, "VATER Syndrome/VACTERL Association," Cincinnati Children's, March 2020, https://www.cincinnatichildrens.org/health/v/vacterl.

34. Herbert Vander Lugt, "The Cure for Resentment," *Our Daily Bread*, September 14, 1995, https://odb.org/US/1995/09/14/the-cure-for-resentment-2.

35. Tyra Bone, greeting card to author's parents, 1995.

36. Robert Fawcett, letter to author's parents, September 20, 1995.

37. CaringBridge, *Quick Facts*, last updated January 2021, https://www.caringbridge.org/wp-content/uploads/2021/04/2021-CaringBridge-Quick-Facts-1.28.21.pdf.

38. Andrea Morris, " 'I Saw the Love of God:' Man Recovers from COVID-19 Life Support, Credits Prayer and Sacrificial Hospital Staff," CBN, April 13, 2020, https://

www1.cbn.com/cbnnews/us/2020/april/i-saw-the-love-of-god-man-recovers-from-covid-19-life-support-credits-prayers-and-sacrificial-hospital-staff.

39. Haven Orecchio-Egresitz, "A Georgia Coronavirus Patient Says He Thought He Was Dying on Wednesday Night. Then He Felt God 'Breathe Life' into His Lungs," *Insider,* March 17, 2020, https://www.insider.com/georgia-man-credits-god-for-recovery-from-coronavirus-2020-3.

40. Randy Travis, "Georgia COVID-19 Victim: 'I feel totally restored now,' " Fox 5 Atlanta, March 20, 2020, https://www.fox5atlanta.com/news/georgia-covid-19-victim-i-feel-totally-restored-now.

41. David Rosenfeld, "Coronavirus Patient's Recovery After 20 days on Ventilator Is a Miracle for Family, a Welcome Boost for Doctors," *Daily Breeze,* April 13, 2020, https://www.dailybreeze.com/2020/04/13/coronavirus-patients-recovery-after-20-days-on-ventilator-is-a-miracle-for-family-a-welcome-boost-for-doctors/.

42. "Colorectal Procedures and Treatments," Children's Hospital Colorado, accessed August 13, 2021, https://www.childrenscolorado.org/doctors-and-departments/departments/colorectal/colorectal-procedures/.

43. "Biliary Atresia," Johns Hopkins Medicine, accessed August 13, 2021, https://www.hopkinsmedicine.org/health/conditions-and-diseases/biliary-atresia.

44. Dr. Alberto Peña, *Monologues of a Pediatric Surgeon* (New York: Dr. Alberto Peña, 2011), 23–25.

45. Peña, 23.

46. Children's Hospital Colorado, "Meet Our Doc: Dr. Alberto Peña," Facebook video, October 14, 2019, https://www.facebook.com/watch/?v=840617573001911.

47. Don K. Nakayama, "Vignettes from the History of Pediatric Surgery," *Journal of Pediatric Surgery* 55 (January 2019): 1–27, https://www.jpedsurg.org/article/S0022-3468(19)30658-X/fulltext#relatedArticles.

48. "Alberto Peña, M.D.," LinkedIn, accessed August 13, 2021, https://www.linkedin.com/in/alberto-pe%C3%B1a-m-d-4277042b.

49. Dr. Alberto Peña, *Monologues of a Pediatric Surgeon* (New York: Dr. Alberto Peña, 2011).

50. Peña, *Monologues of a Pediatric Surgeon,* 26.

51. Children's Hospital Colorado, "World-Renowned Colorectal Pediatric Surgeons Join Children's Hospital Colorado," PR Newswire, February 18, 2016, https://www.prnewswire.com/news-releases/world-renowned-colorectal-pediatric-surgeons-join-childrens-hospital-colorado-300222722.html.

52. Tessa Koumoundouros, "It Pays to Be Kind. People Live Longer in Societies That Share More Across Generations," *ScienceAlert,* September 6, 2020, https://www.sciencealert.com/people-live-longer-in-societies-that-share-more-across-generations.

53. Shruti Pillai, "Did You Know That Farting in Front of Your Partner Is a Sign of a Mature, Strong Relationship?," *ScoopWhoop,* March 18, 2016, https://www.scoopwhoop.com/Farting-In-Front-Of-Your-Partner-Relationship-Success/.

54. "Old Club," Detroit Historical Society, accessed August 13, 2021, https://detroithistorical.pastperfectonline.com/bysearchterm?keyword=Old+Club.

55. "Lake St. Clair," New Baltimore, Michigan, accessed August 13, 2021, https://www.newbaltimoremi.com/lake-st-clair-new-baltimore-mi.

56. Michael Inbar, " 'Groundhog Day' for Real: Woman Stuck in 1994," *TODAY*, August 16, 2010, https://www.today.com/news/groundhog-day-real-woman-stuck-1994-1C9017393.

57. Arlin Cuncic, "What Is Anterograde Amnesia?," *Verywell Mind*, April 8, 2020, https://www.verywellmind.com/an-overview-of-anterograde-amnesia-4581313.

58. Andrew Levy, "The Woman Who Wakes Up Thinking It's 1994 Every Morning and Then Forgets Everything the Next Day Due to Car Crash Injury," *Daily Mail*, June 10, 2010, https://www.dailymail.co.uk/health/article-1285535/Two-car-crashes-leave-Michelle-Philpots-24-hour-memory.html.

59. Mother Goose, "Jack and Jill," Poetry Foundation, accessed August 13, 2021, https://www.poetryfoundation.org/poems/46974/jack-and-jill-56d2271cb3535.

60. Mother Goose, "Humpty Dumpty Sat on a Wall," Poetry Foundation, accessed August 13, 2021, https://www.poetryfoundation.org/poems/46951/humpty-dumpty-sat-on-a-wall.

61. "Our School: Legacy," University Liggett School, accessed August 13, 2021, https://uls.org/our-school/legacy/.

62. *Finding Dory*, directed by Andrew Stanton, featuring Ellen DeGeneres (Emryville, CA: Pixar, 2016), DVD, 10:18.

63. Nina Bai, "Still Confused About Masks? Here's the Science Behind How Face Masks Prevent Coronavirus," University of California San Francisco, June 26, 2020, https://www.ucsf.edu/news/2020/06/417906/still-confused-about-masks-heres-science-behind-how-face-masks-prevent.

64. "Our Founder," Tattum Reading (website), accessed August 13, 2021, http://www.tattumreading.com/our-founder.html.

65. "Book Series," Tattum Reading (website), accessed August 13, 2021, http://www.tattumreading.com/books.html.

66. Evan Andrews, "10 Things You May Not Know About F. Scott Fitzgerald," HISTORY, August 31, 2018, https://www.history.com/news/10-things-you-may-not-know-about-f-scott-fitzgerald.

67. Dylan Love, "15 CEOs with Learning Disabilities," *Insider*, May 19, 2011, https://www.businessinsider.com/ceo-learning-disabilities-2011-5.

68. "Steven Spielberg Escaped His Dyslexia Through Filmmaking," ABC News, September 27, 2012, https://abcnews.go.com/blogs/entertainment/2012/09/steven-spielberg-escaped-his-dyslexia-through-filmmaking.

69. "Dyslexia Basics," International Dyslexia Association, March 10, 2020. https://dyslexiaida.org/dyslexia-basics/.

70. Andrew M. I. Lee, "The 13 Disability Categories Under IDEA," Understood, accessed August 18, 2021, https://www.understood.org/articles/en/conditions-covered-under-idea.

71. "Dyslexia Basics."

72. "Dyslexia Basics."

73. "Dyslexia Basics."

74. Emily Friedman, "Dyspraxia Explains Harry Potter's Klutziness," ABC News, August 19, 2008, https://abcnews.go.com/Health/story?id=5605093.

75. WSJ Staff, "21 Random Questions with Daniel Radcliffe," *The Wall Street Journal*,

October 28, 2014, https://www.wsj.com/articles/BL-SEB-84461.

76. "Tim Tebow," Heisman Trophy, accessed August 18, 2021, https://www.heisman.com/heisman-winners/tim-tebow/.

77. Brian Costello, "Dyslexia Could Never Sack Tebow," *New York Post*, August 3, 2012, https://nypost.com/2012/08/03/dyslexia-could-never-sack-tebow/.

78. Costello.

79. Costello.

80. Taylor Locke, "Barbara Corcoran: How Dyslexia 'Made Me a Millionaire,' " *Make It,* CNBC, March 10, 2020, last updated January 12, 2021, https://www.cnbc.com/2020/03/10/barbara-corcoran-how-dyslexia-made-me-a-millionaire.html.

81. Kim Lachance Shandrow, "How Being Dyslexic and 'Lousy in School' Made Shark Tank Star Barbara Corcoran a Better Entrepreneur," *Entrepreneur,* September 19, 2014, https://www.entrepreneur.com/article/237669.

82. Shivaune Field, "Barbara Corcoran On Dyslexia, The Power of Empathy and Oprah as President," *Forbes,* February 1, 2018, https://www.forbes.com/sites/shivaunefield/2018/01/31barbara-corcoran-on-dyslexia-the-power-of-empathy-and-oprah-as-president/.

83. Benjamin Snyder, "Here Are 5 Business Leaders Who Live with Dyslexia," *Fortune,* October 15, 2015, https://fortune.com/2015/10/15/business-leaders-dyslexia/.

84. Kevin O'Leary, *Cold Hard Truth: On Business, Money & Life* (Toronto, Ontario: Doubleday Canada, 2011).

85. Kim Lachance Shandrow, "Shark Tank's Kevin O'Leary: Having Dyslexia Is a 'Superpower' in Business," *Entrepreneur,* June 22, 2016, https://www.entrepreneur.com/article/277911.

86. Julie Logan, "Dyslexic Entrepreneurs: The Incidence; Their Coping Strategies and Their Business Skills," *Dyslexia* 15, no. 4 (2009): 328–46, https://doi.org/10.1002/dys.388.

87. Theresa Johnston, "Charles Schwab's Secret Struggle," *Stanford Magazine,* March/April 1999, https://stanfordmag.org/contents/charles-schwab-s-secret-struggle.

88. "Investor Relations," Charles Schwab Corporation, accessed August 18, 2021, https://aboutschwab.com/investor-relations.

89. Kalani Simpson, "Anthony Robles' 'Unstoppable' Drive," ESPN, July 12, 2011, http://www.espn.com/espn/page2/story?id=6754598.

90. "About Me," Anthony Robles (website), accessed August 18, 2021, https://anthonyrobles.com/about.

91. "Anthony Robles," National Wrestling Hall of Fame, accessed August 18, 2021, https://nwhof.org/hall_of_fame/bio/2517.

92. Shannon Cross, "Q&A: Anthony Robles," ESPN, August 19, 2012, https://www.espn.com/espn/story/_/id/7833398/qa-national-wrestling-champion-anthony-robles.

93. Samantha Grossman, "This Simple Trick Turns Sliced Apples into a Super Portable Snack," *TIME,* April 30, 2021, https://time.com/3842414/apple-slice-rubber-band-life-hack/.

94. Alina Bradford, "Remove a Stripped Screw in Seconds Using a Rubber Band," CNET, February 12, 2016, https://www.cnet.com/home/kitchen-and-household/remove-a-stripped-screw-in-seconds-with-this-office-supply/.

95. Meagan Nielsen, "The Rubberband Maternity Trick," *DIY Maternity,* September 27, 2010, http://diymaternity.com/pants-skirts/the-rubberband-maternity-trick/.

96. Meng-Fai Kuo et al., "Tethered Spinal Cord and VACTERL Association," *Journal of Neurosurgery* 106, no. 3 (March 2007): https://doi.org/10.3171/ped.2007.106.3.201.

97. "Tethered Spinal Cord Syndrome Information Page," National Institute of Neurological Disorders and Stroke, last updated March 27, 2019, https://ninds.nih.gov/Disorders/All-Disorders/Tethered-Spinal-Cord-Syndrome-Information-Page.

98. "Tethered Spinal Cord Syndrome Information Page."

99. Mayo Clinic Staff, "Chiari Malformation," Mayo Clinic, September 12, 2019, https://www.mayoclinic.org/diseases-conditions/chiari-malformation/symptoms-causes/syc-20354010.

100. Jeffrey A. Steinberg et al, "Spinal Shortening for Recurrent Tethered Cord Syndrome via a Lateral Retropleural Approach: A Novel Operative Technique," *Cureus* 9, no. 8 (August 2017), https://www.ncbi.nlm.nih.gov/pmc/articles/PMC5663326/.

101. Antoinette Martin and Darryl Fears, "Rainbow's End," *Detroit Free Press,* November 22, 1987, 133.

102. Martin and Fears.

103. Martin and Fears.

104. "History of the University," High Point University, accessed August 23, 2021, https://www.highpoint.edu/visitorinformation/history-of-the-university/.

105. "Dr. Qubein Biography," Office of the President, High Point University, accessed August 23, 2021, https://www.highpoint.edu/president/dr-qubein-biography/.

106. Marla Horn Lazarus,, "Nido Qubein, President of High Point University, Blessed with Faithful Courage," *Authority Magazine, Medium,* December 4, 2018, https://medium.com/authority-magazine/nido-qubein-president-of-high-point-university-blessed-with-faithful-courage-ebbbaddf887a.

107. "Nido R. Qubein | A Live of Success and Significance | High Point University," aired September 2013, on the Biography Channel, video shared by High Point University, January 30, 2015, on YouTube, 1:25, https://www.youtube.com/watch?v=kQf6WTtzSGc&ab_channel=HighPointUniversity.

108. "Nido R. Qubein," 1:48.

109. "Nido R. Qubein," 2:00.

110. Azim Jamal, and Nido R. Qubein, *Life Balance: The Sufi Way* (Mumbai, India: Jaico Publishing House, 2007), 138–39.

111. "Nido R. Qubein," 3:00.

112. Jamal and Qubein, *Life Balance: The Sufi Way,* 141.

113. Azriel Reshel, "Sufi Teachings to Light Your Way," *UPLIFT,* accessed August 23, 2021, https://uplift.love/sufi-teachings-to-light-your-way/.

114. Karen Stevens, "Making the Grade," *SUCCESS,* September 2012, 41, https://www.highpoint.edu/president/files/2012/10/success-magazine-sept-2012.pdf.

115. "Nido R. Qubein," 3:55

116. John Brasier, "BB&T Board Member Qubein Says Merger Was Best for Bank, Triad Jobs," *Triad Business Journal,* February 7, 2019, https://www.bizjournals.com/triad/news/2019/02/07/bb-t-board-member-qubein-says-merger-was-best-for.html.

117. Jamal and Qubein, *Life Balance the Sufi Way*.

118. Reggie Ugwu and Michael Levenson, " 'Black Panther' Star Chadwick Boseman Dies of Cancer at 43," *The New York Times*, August 28, 2020, https://www.nytimes.com/2020/08/28/movies/chadwick-boseman-dead.html.

119. Christi Carras, "Denzel Washington Honors His Special Bond with Chadwick Boseman," *Los Angeles Times*, August 31, 2020, https://latimes.com/entertainment-arts/story/2020-08-31/chadwick-boseman-death-denzel-washington-tribute.

120. Carras.

121. Joe Gyan Jr., "Warrick Dunn: Mother's Killers No Longer Have 'Power Over Me or My Family,' " *Advocate*, September 28, 2018, https://www.theadvocate.com/baton_rouge/news/courts/article_155833fa-c1bd-11e8-9984-a70b05270caa.html.

122. Michael David Smith, "Warrick Dunn Opens Up About the Lingering Effects of His Mother's Murder," Pro Football Talk, NBC Sports, June 28, 2019, https://profootballtalk.nbcsports.com/2019/06/28/warrick-dunn-opens-up-about-the-lingering-effects-of-his-mothers-murder/.

123. "Meet Our Founder," Warrick Dunn Charities, accessed August 23, 2021, https://wdc.org/about-our-founder/.

124. "Meet Our Founder."

125. Perry Kostidakis, "First Is the Sweetest: The 1993 National Champs," *FSU News*, January 23, 2015, fsunews.com/story/sports/college/fsu/football/2015/01/23/first-sweetest-national-champs/22222983/.

126. "Meet Our Founder," Warrick Dunn Charities.

127. "Meet Our Founder."

128. "Homes for the Holidays," Warrick Dunn Charities, accessed August 23, 2021, https://wdc.org/homes-for-the-holidays/.

129. Richard L. Evans, *Richard Evans' Quote Book* (Salt Lake City, UT: Publishers Press, 1971), 244.

130. Justin W. Patchin and Sameer Hinduja, "2019 Cyberbullying Data," Cyberbullying Research Center, July 9, 2019, https://cyberbullying.org/2019-cyberbullying-data.

131. "Social Media Fact Sheet," Pew Research Center, April 7, 2021, https://www.pewresearch.org/internet/fact-sheet/social-media/.

132. "Social Media Fact Sheet."

133. Statista Research Department, "Number of Social Network Users Worldwide from 2017 to 2025," *Statista*, January 28, 2021, https://www.statista.com/statistics/278414/number-of-worldwide-social-network-users/.

134. Beth Shilliday, "Cindy Crawford, 54, Recalls How Her 1st Modeling Agency Asked Her to Remove Her Famous Beauty Mark," *Hollywood Life*, April 7, 2020, https://hollywoodlife.com/2020/04/07/cindy-crawford-asked-to-remove-beauty-mark-interview-video/.

135. Pat Forde, "Michael Phelps Turns Tables on Childhood Bullies," Yahoo! News, July 27, 2012, https://www.yahoo.com/news/olympics--michael-phelps-turns-tables-on-childhood-bullies.html.

136. Louise Gannon, "Jessica Alba: 'I'd Definitely Go for the Shy, Nerdy Type of Guy,' " *Daily Mail*, October 27, 2007, https://www.dailymail.co.uk/home/moslive/article-489884/Jessica-Alba-Id-definitely-shy-nerdy-type-guy.html.

137. Julie Mazziotta, "Blake Lively Opens Up About Being Bullied for Her Height: Kids Were 'Calling Me Big Bird.' " *People*, April 17, 2018, https://people.com/health/blake-lively-bullied-height-calling-me-big-bird/.

138. Justin Timberlake, "Web Exclusive: Justin Timberlake on Bullying" (interview with Ellen Degeneres, Warner Bros. Studios, Burbank, California), video shared by TheEllenShow, November 22, 2010, on YouTube, https://www.youtube.com/watch?v=JLhvTcEWbEg&ab_channel=TheEllenShow.

139. Samantha Grossman, "Read the Uplifting Message Taylor Swift Wrote to a Fan Who's Struggling with Bullies," *TIME*, September 5, 2014, https://time.com/3273740/taylor-swift-instagram-comments-bullied-fan/.

140. Marie Fazio, "An Italian Teenager Could Become the First Millennial Saint," *The New York Times*, October 12, 2020, https://www.nytimes.com/2020/10/12/world/europe/millennial-saint-carlo-acutis.html.

141. Sam Lucero, "A Model for Young People," *The Compass*, October 14, 2020, https://www.thecompassnews.org/2020/10/a-model-for-young-people/.

142. Fazio, "An Italian Teenager Could Become the First Millennial Saint."

143. Courtney Mares, "Beautification of Carlo Acutis: The First Millennial Is Declared 'Blessed,' " *National Catholic Register*, October 10, 2020, https://www.ncregister.com/news/beatification-of-carlo-acutis-the-first-millennial-is-declared-blessed.

144. Fazio, "An Italian Teenager Could Become the First Millennial Saint."

145. Courtney Mares, "Carlo Acutis Loved the Homeless, St. Francis of Assisi, and Souls in Purgatory," Catholic News Agency, October 7, 2020, https://www.catholicnewsagency.com/news/46124/carlo-acutis-loved-the-homeless-st-francis-of-assisi-and-souls-in-purgatory.

146. Fazio, "An Italian Teenager Could Become the First Millennial Saint."

147. The Holy Father Francis, *Christus Vivit* (post-synodal apostolic exhortation, Shrine of the Holy House, Loreto, Italy, March 25, 2019), Liberia Editrice Vaticana, http://www.vatican.va/content/francesco/en/apost_exhortations/documents/papa-francesco_esortazione-ap_20190325_christus-vivit.html.

148. Fazio, "An Italian Teenager Could Become the First Millennial Saint."

149. Fazio.

150. Junno Arocho Esteves, "Beautified Teen Showed That Heaven Is 'Attainable Goal,' the Cardinal Says," Catholic News Service, October 10, 2020, https://www.catholicnews.com/beatified-teen-showed-that-heaven-is-attainable-goal-cardinal-says/.

151. CNA Staff, "The Miracle Attributed to Carlo Acutis' Prayers," Catholic News Agency, October 10, 2020, https://www.catholicnewsagency.com/news/the-miracle-attributed-to-carlo-acutis-prayers-95939.

152. CNA Staff.

153. CNA Staff.

154. Fazio, "An Italian Teenager Could Become the First Millennial Saint."

155. "Joan of Arc Is Burned at the Stake for Heresy," HISTORY, November 24, 2009, https://www.history.com/this-day-in-history/joan-of-arc-martyred.

156. Ryan McGee, "Rex Chapman Is a Comeback Story and a Twitter Feed for Our Time," ESPN, March 26, 2020, https://www.espn.com/mens-college-basketball/story/_/id/28958919/rex-chapman-comeback-story-twitter-feed-our.

157. "Rex Chapman," Kentucky High School Basketball Hall of Fame, February 8, 2018, https://khsbhf.com/rex-chapman/.

158. Brian Jones, "Rex Chapman: What to Know About the NBA Player Turned Twitter Influencer," *Pop Culture*, November 17, 2020, https://popculture.com/sports/news/john-cena-reveals-dwayne-the-rock-johnson-should-return-wwe/.

159. Jones, "Rex Chapman: What to Know About the NBA Player Turned Twitter Influencer."

160. McGee, "Rex Chapman Is a Comeback Story and a Twitter Feed for Our Time."

161. McGee.

162. McGee.

163. Rex Chapman (@RexChapman), "This groom surprised his new bride," Twitter, January 11, 2021, 11:42 a.m., https://twitter.com/RexChapman/status/1348671536954273793.

164. Rex Chapman (@RexChapman), "Her son has cerebral palsy, but he's always wanted to skateboard," Twitter, July 1, 2020, https://twitter.com/RexChapman/status/1278391075657433089.

165. Rex Chapman (@RexChapman), Twitter, March 11, 2020, 12:08 p.m., https://twitter.com/RexChapman/status/1237772372041773057.

166. McGee, "Rex Chapman Is a Comeback Story and a Twitter Feed for Our Time."

167. Starr Bowenbank, "Shawn Mendes Talks Learning How to Play Guitar & Opening for Taylor Swift on Spotify Podcast," *Billboard*, November 15, 2018, https://www.billboard.com/articles/columns/pop/8485291/shawn-mendes-interview-spotify-guy-raz-podcast.

168. Associated Press, "Shawn Mendes on Leap from Vine Star to Major Label Target: 'It Was Absolutely Insane,' " *Billboard*, July 23, 2014, https://www.billboard.com/articles/columns/pop-shop/6176073/shawn-mendes-on-leap-from-vine-star-to-major-label-target-it-was.

169. Shawn Mendes (@shawnmendes), "I'm thinking about being in 9th grade right now," Instagram, June 23, 2019, https://www.instagram.com/p/BzESroPHYMB/?utm_source=ig_embed&ig_rid=49ee0598-0762-45bb-b3ac-bb4d21a2451e.

170. Gary Trust, "Shawn Mendes Is First Artist in AC Chart's History to Notch Three No. 1s Before Age 20," *Billboard*, November 7, 2017, https://www.billboard.com/articles/business/chart-beat/8023330/shawn-mendes-ac-chart-three-number-ones-before-age-20/.

171. Gary Trust, "Shawn Mendes Is the First Artist to Land Four No. 1s on the Adult Pop Songs Chart Before Age 20," *Billboard*, July 31, 2018, https://www.billboard.com/articles/columns/chart-beat/8467895/shawn-mendes-first-artist-to-have-four-no-1s-adult-pop-songs.

172. Keith Caulfield, "Shawn Mendes Achieves Fourth No. 1 Album on Billboard 200 Chart with 'Wonder,' " *Billboard*, December 13, 2020, https://www.billboard.com/articles/business/chart-beat/9498963/shawn-mendes-wonder-tops-billboard-200-chart/.

173. "'Be Kind to Everyone,' Says Shawn Mendes," CBC News, 2017, 0:26, https://www.cbc.ca/player/play/912812099772.

174. "Shawn Mendes and Camila Cabello Surprise Healthcare Workers in Miami with Cuban Sandwiches," ABC News Radio, April 15, 2020, http://abcnewsradioonline.com/music-news/2020/4/15/shawn-mendes-and-camila-cabello-surprise-healthcare-workers.html.

175. Andy Kopsa, "What to Know About Czechoslovakia's Velvet Revolution," *TIME*, November 16, 2019, https://time.com/5730106/velvet-revolution-history/.

176. Kopsa, "What to Know About Czechoslovakia's Velvet Revolution."

177. Vishu Vishwabramana, "Story of an Eagle," *Times of India Reader's Blog*, July 27, 2020, https://timesofindia.indiatimes.com/readersblog/vishwabramana/story-of-an-eagle-23667/.

178. "Bald Eagle," *National Geographic*, accessed August 23, 2021, https://www.nationalgeographic.com/animals/birds/b/bald-eagle/.

179. "Learn About Eagles: Eagle Biology," National Eagle Center, accessed August 23, 2021, https://www.nationaleaglecenter.org/learn/biology/.

180. Vishwabramana, "Story of an Eagle."

181. Understood Team, "7 Things to Know About College Disability Services," accessed August 26, 2021, https://www.understood.org/articles/en/7-things-to-know-about-college-disability-services.

182. Kendra Graham, "I'm Making Pearls in Here!," *Decision*, October 11, 2018, https://decisionmagazine.com/im-making-pearls-here/.

183. Graham.

184. Graham.

185. Josh Groban, "High Point University 2018 Commencement" (commencement speech, High Point University, High Point, North Carolina, May 5, 2018), video shared by High Point University, May 16, 2018, on YouTube, https://www.youtube.com/watch?v=f155JYqlr3A&ab_channel=HighPointUniversity.

186. Groban, 1:25.

187. Adam Hetrick, "Josh Groban Talks Dream Roles, Studio Time with Audra McDonald and Why Rap Is in His Future," *Playbill*, May 7, 2015, https://www.playbill.com/article/josh-groban-talks-dream-roles-studio-time-with-audra-mcdonald-and-why-rap-is-in-his-future-com-348472.

188. Groban, 9:08.

189. Groban, 9:37.

190. Groban, 11:13.

191. Groban, 13:38.

192. Groban, 16:48.

193. Groban, 22:13.

194. Groban, 23:40.

195. Groban, 31:55, from Stephen Sondheim, "Move On," track 15 on *Sunday in the Park with George*, RCA, July 1, 1984.

196. "Timeline," *Guinness World Records*, accessed August 28, 2021, https://www.guinnessworldrecords.com/about-us/our-history/timeline.

197. "Our History," *Guinness World Records*, accessed August 28, 2021, https://www.guinnessworldrecords.com/about-us/our-history.

198. "Porsche Taycan Drifts into the Guinness World Records™ Book," Newsroom, November 23, 2020, https://newsroom.porsche.com/en_US/products/porsche-taycan-drift-record-guinness-world-records-book-22949.html.

199. *Guinness World Records*, s.v., "Farthest Arrow Shot Using Feet," March 31, 2018, https://www.guinnessworldrecords.com/world-records/74687-farthest-arrow -shot-using-feet.

200. *Guinness World Records*, s.v., "Most Toothpicks in a Beard," July 7, 2018, https://www.guinnessworldrecords.com/world-records/104435-most-toothpicks-in-a-beard.

201. *Guinness World Records*, s.v., "Highest Jump on a Pogo Stick," November 20, 2018, https://www.guinnessworldrecords.com/world-records/highest-jump-on-a-pogo-stick.

202. Connie Suggitt, "Teen's Hair Reaches Two Metres Making It the Longest Ever," *Guinness World Records*, November 4, 2020, https://www.guinness-worldrecords.com/news/2020/11/teens-hair-reaches-two-metres-making-it-the -longest-ever-636656.

203. *Guinness World Records*, s.v. "Largest Hula Hoop Spun (Female)," November 2, 2018, https://www.guinnessworldrecords.com/world-records/553221-largest-hu-la-hoop -spun-female.

204. *Guinness World Records*, s.v., "Most Consecutive Pinky Pull-Ups," October 7, 2018, https://www.guinnessworldrecords.com/world-records/most-consecutive -pinky-pull-ups.

205. *Guinness World Records*, s.v., "Fastest Time to Eat a Bowl of Pasta," September 18, 2017, https://www.guinnessworldrecords.com/world-records/fastest-time-to-eat-a-bowl-of-pasta.

206. *Guinness World Records*, s.v., "Most Piercings, Single Count (Female)," May 4, 2000, https://www.guinnessworldrecords.com/world-records/most-piercings -single-count-(female).

207. *Guinness World Records*, "Most Big Mac' Burgers Eaten in a Lifetime," August 24, 2016, https://www.guinnessworldrecords.com/world-records/most-big -macs-consumed.

208. Connie Suggitt, " 'I'm No Different to Anyone Else'—Meet Lucky Diamond Rich, The World's Most Tattooed Man," *Guinness World Records*, August 5, 2019, https://www.guinnessworldrecords.com/news/book/2019/8/im-no-different-to-anyone-else-meet-lucky-diamond-rich-the-worlds-most-tatto-585598.

209. "Kilimanjaro Geology," Climbing Kilimanjaro, accessed August 28, 2021, https://www.climbing-kilimanjaro.com/kilimanjaro-geology/.

210. "Kilimanjaro," *National Geographic*, September 20, 2019, https://www.national-geographic.org/encyclopedia/kilimanjaro/.

211. Bill Porter, "100 Miles to Glory: Tanzanian Ultramarathoner a Runner with a Mission," *Valley News,* July 19, 2015, https://www.vnews.com/Archives/2015/07/mtuy-bp-vn-071915.

212. "About Us: Simon Mtuy," Summit Expeditions & Nomadic Experience, accessed August 28, 2021, https://www.nomadicexperience.com/about-us/simon-mtuy/.

213. Porter, "100 Miles to Glory."

214. Simon Mtuy, "Speedy Simon!," Kilimanjaro Stage Run, January 10, 2019, https://kilimanjarostagerun.com/speedy-simon/; Christopher Solomon, "Becoming the

All-Terrain Human," *New York Times Magazine*, March 20, 2013. https://www.nytimes.com/2013/03/24/magazine/creating-the-all-terrrain-human.html.

215. Porter, "100 Miles to Glory."

216. Mtuy, "Speedy Simon!"

217. "HIV and AIDS in Tanzania," Avert.org, last updated March 19, 2020, https://www.avert.org/professionals/hiv-around-world/sub-saharan-africa/tanzania.

218. "Simon Mtuy," Kilimanjaro Stage Run, accessed August 28, 2021, https://kilimanjarostagerun.com/inspiration/simon-mtuy/.

219. "Myths and Mysteries of Mount Kilimanjaro," Just Kilimanjaro, accessed August 28, 2021, http://www.just-kilimanjaro.com/?/blog/view/myths-and-mysteries-of-mount-kilimanjaro.

220. Michaela Trimble, "How to Hike and Climb Kilimanjaro," REI, October 31, 2018, https://www.rei.com/blog/travel/how-to-travel-to-and-climb-kilimanjaro.

221. "Umbwe Route," Climbing Kilimanjaro, accessed August 28, 2021, https://www.climbing-kilimanjaro.com/umbwe-route/.

222. "Umbwe Route—Kilimanjaro," Tourradar, accessed August 28, 2021, https://www.tourradar.com/hg/umbwe-route.

223. "Kilimanjaro Success Rates—How Many People Reach the Summit," Climb Kilimanjaro Guide, last updated June 16, 2021, https://www.climbkilimanjaroguide.com/kilimanjaro-success-rate/.

224. "Umbwe Route," Ultimate Kilimanjaro, accessed August 28, 2021, https://www.ultimatekilimanjaro.com/umbwe_route.htm.

225. "Climbing Mt. Kilimanjaro via the Western Breach Route," Mount Kilimanjaro Guide, accessed August 29, 2021, https://www.mountkilimanjaroguide.com/kilimanjaro-western-breach.html.

226. "Climbing Mt. Kilimanjaro via the Western Breach Route."

227. "Pole Pole! Go Slow and Connect," *Tanzania Blog*, Summit Expeditions & Nomadic Experience, September 13, 2018, https://www.nomadicexperience.com/slowtravel/.

228. Stephanie Thurrott, "What You Need to Know About Your Blood Oxygen Level," Banner Health, accessed August 28, 2021, https://www.bannerhealth.com/healthcareblog/teach-me/blood-oxygen-level-what-you-need-to-know.

229. "Climbs Resources," Summit Expeditions & Nomadic Experience, accessed August 28, 2021, https://www.nomadicexperience.com/climbs/resources-climbs/.

230. James Balog, "Tragedy on Kilimanjaro," *National Geographic,* August 2, 2016, https://www.nationalgeographic.com/adventure/article/kilimanjaro-breach-climbing-death.

231. David DeBolt, "East Bay Entrepreneur, Author Scott Dinsmore Killed While Climbing Mount Kilimanjaro" *Mercury News,* August 12, 2016, https://www.mercurynews.com/2015/09/15/east-bay-entrepreneur-author-scott-dinsmore-killed-while-climbing-mount-kilimanjaro/.

232. "Climbing Mt. Kilimanjaro via the Western Breach Route."

233. "Global Ostomy Drainage Bags Market $4.1 Billion by 2027," iHealthcareAnalyst, June 28, 2021, https://www.ihealthcareanalyst.com/global-ostomy-drainage-bags-market/.

234. "What Makes a Guinness World Records Title?," *Guinness World Records,* accessed August 28, 2021, guinnessworldrecords.com/records/what-makes-a-guinness-world-records-record-title.

235. "What Makes a Guinness World Records Title?"

236. "What Makes a Guinness World Records Title?"

237. Marguerite Ward, "Warren Buffett's Reading Routine Could Make You Smarter, Science Suggests," *Make It,* November 16, 2016, https://www.cnbc.com/2016/11/16/warren-buffetts-reading-routine-could-make-you-smarter-suggests-science.html.

238. Marguerite Ward, "What 9 Self-Made Millionaires Do Before Breakfast," *Make It,* September 6, 2016, https://www.cnbc.com/2016/09/06/what-9-self-made-millionaires-do-before-breakfast.html.

239. Marcel Schwantes, "Warren Buffett Says Anyone Can Achieve Success By Following 1 Simple Formula He Uses Every Day," *Inc.,* February 10, 2020, https://www.inc.com/marcel-schwantes/warren-buffett-says-anyone-can-achieve-success-by-following-1-simple-formula-he-uses-every-day.html.

240. "#6 Warren Buffett," *Forbes,* last updated August 29, 2021, https://www.forbes.com/profile/warren-buffett/?sh=6ae5f5674639.

241. Steve Jordon, "Investors Earn Handsome Paychecks By Handling Buffett's Business," *Omaha World-Herald,* April 28, 2013, https://omaha.com/business/investors-earn-handsome-paychecks-by-handling-buffett-s-business/article_bb1fc40f-e6f9-549d-be2f-be1ef4c0da03.html.

242. Ben Hanback, "What Will You Learn after You Know It All?," *The Tennessean,* January 3, 2016, https://www.tennessean.com/story/money/2016/01/03/what-you-learn-after-you-know-all/78108188/.

243. Steve Carter, "Start Building Meaningful Relationships!," interview by JT Jester, video shared by JTJesterSpeaks, April 28, 2020, on YouTube, 1:29, https://www.youtube.com/watch?v=2_Kmls5DQyA&t=7s&ab_channel=JTJesterSpeaks.

244. Carter, 1:59.

245. Carter, 4:19.

246. Carter, 6:12.

247. Carter, 7:40.

248. Nick Strand, "Leave Your Comfort Zone Behind Now!," interview by JT Jester, video shared by JTJesterSpeaks, September 5, 2020, on YouTube, 1:21, https://www.youtube.com/watch?v=Vu5Uc1b-J3M&ab_channel=JTJesterSpeaks.

249. "About Cystic Fibrosis," Cystic Fibrosis Foundation, accessed August 30, 2021, https://www.cff.org/What-is-CF/About-Cystic-Fibrosis/.

250. Christian Voster, "Cystic Fibrosis Walk Part of Poulsbo Woman's Legacy," *Kitsap Sun,* May 31, 2017, https://www.kitsapsun.com/story/news/local/communities/north-kitsap/2017/05/31/cystic-fibrosis-walk-part-poulsbo-womans-legacy/359686001/.

251. Richard Walker, "She Served Until the Very End," *Kitsap Daily News,* May 11, 2017, https://www.kitsapdailynews.com/news/she-served-until-the-very-end/.

252. Voster, "Cystic Fibrosis Walk Part of Poulsbo Woman's Legacy."

253. "Brianna Oas and Nick Strand | Engagements," *Kitsap Daily*

News, June 22, 2011, https://www.kitsapdailynews.com/life/brianna-oas-and-nick-strand-engagements/.

254. Strand, "Leave Your Comfort Zone Behind Now!," 1:27.

255. Walker, "She Served Until the Very End."

256. Voster, "Cystic Fibrosis Walk Part of Poulsbo Woman's Legacy."

257. Walker.

258. Strand, "Leave Your Comfort Zone Behind Now!," 3:44.

259. Strand, 8:52.

260. Strand, 5:00.

261. "Nicholas Strand," Choose Your Attitude, accessed August 30, 2021, https://chooseyourattitude.com/pages/nicholas.

262. "Facts About Hypoplastic Left Heart Syndrome," Centers for Disease Control and Prevention, November 17, 2020, https://www.cdc.gov/ncbddd/heartdefects/hlhs.html.

263. Daniel Foy, "Born with Half a Heart | Keeping the Right Perspective," interview by JT Jester, video shared by JTJesterSpeaks, April 15, 2020, on YouTube, 1:32, https://www.youtube.com/watch?v=yW4a3W4IEFg&ab_channel=JTJesterSpeaks.

264. Foy, 1:42.

265. Foy, 2:50.

266. "Plastic Bronchitis," Penn Medicine, Causes and Symptoms, accessed August 30, 2021, https://www.pennmedicine.org/for-patients-and-visitors/patient-information/conditions-treated-a-to-z/plastic-bronchitis.

267. Foy, "Born with Half a Heart," 4:05.

268. Foy, 9:40.

269. Foy, 8:13.

270. Foy, 10:47.

271. Foy, 13:33.

272. Aaron Boyd, "Why We Do What We Do," interview by JT Jester, video shared by JTJesterSpeaks, April 6, 2020, on YouTube, 0:49, https://www.youtube.com/watch?v=5t-d24vHMm8&ab_channel=JTJesterSpeaks.

273. Boyd, 4:51.

274. "Featured Artist: Bluetree," Louder Than the Music, April 1, 2009, https://www.louderthanthemusic.com/document.php?id=142.

275. Boyd, 9:44, 14:04.

276. Rina Chandran, "In Thai Tourist Spots, a Hidden World of Male Sex Slavery," Reuters, June 13, 2018, https://www.reuters.com/article/us-thailand-trafficking-sexcrimes/in-thai-tourist-spots-a-hidden-world-of-male-sex-slavery-idUSKBN1J91GU.

277. "Anti-Human Trafficking and Child Abuse Center Needs Urgent Help," *Pattaya Mail*, January 26, 2020, https://www.pattayamail.com/news/anti-human-trafficking-and-child-abuse-center-needs-urgent-help-285580.

278. Boyd, "Why We Do What We Do," 11:24.

279. Boyd, 15:18.

280. Boyd, 15:47.

281. Boyd, 13:06.

282. Boyd, 16:07.

283. "God of This City by Chris Tomlin," Songfacts, 2017, https://www.songfacts.com/facts/chris-tomlin/god-of-this-city.

284. Boyd, 17:02.

285. "Partner with Us," Aaron Boyd Music, https://www.aaronboydmusic.com/partner .

286. YoungMin You, "Nothing Is Impossible," interview by JT Jester, video shared by JTJesterSpeaks, April 27, 2020, on YouTube, 1:24, https://www.youtube.com/watch?v=Me81x_GCxjc&ab_channel=JTJesterSpeaks.

287. You, 2:30.

288. You, 3:14.

289. You, 3:52.

290. You, 5:40.

291. You, 6:15.

292. You, 6:47.

293. You, 7:25.

294. You, 8:07.

295. You, 8:14.

296. You, 9:24.

297. Emily Haines Lloyd, "YoungMin You: Beating the Odds," *Michigan Country Lines*, December 2019, https://www.countrylines.com/cover-story/youngmin-you-beating-the-odds/.

298. You, 8:23.

299. Lloyd, "YoungMin You: Beating the Odds."

300. YoungMin You, YouTube channel, accessed August 30, 2021, https://www.youtube.com/c/youngminyou/about.

301. Scott Burgess, "Detroit's Production Battle to Win World War III," *Motortrend*, May 28, 2018, https://www.motortrend.com/features/detroits-production-battle-to-win-world-war-ii/.

302. A. J. Baime, "How Detroit Factories Retooled During WWII to Defeat Hitler," HISTORY, March 19, 2020, https://www.history.com/news/wwii-detroit-auto-factories-retooled-homefront.

303. "The Great Migration (1910–1970)," National Archives, June 28, 2021, https://www.archives.gov/research/african-americans/migrations/great-migration.

304. *The Second Great Migration*, National Geographic Education (Washington, DC: National Geographic Society, 2012), 1, https://media.nationalgeographic.org/assets/file/african_american_MIG.pdf.

305. "Arsenal of Democracy," Encyclopedia of Detroit, Detroit Historical Society, accessed November 16, 2020, https://detroithistorical.org/learn/encyclopedia-of-detroit/arsenal-democracy.

306. Marion F. Wilson, *The Story of Willow Run* (University of Michigan Press, 1956).

307. Encyclopedia.com, s.v., "Chateau Communities, Inc.," accessed August 30, 2021, https://www.encyclopedia.com/books/politics-and-business-magazines/chateau-communities-inc.

308. "The Boll Legacy," The John A. and Marlene L. Boll Foundation, accessed November 16, 2020, http://www.bollfoundation.org/about.html.

309. "About," JT Mestdagh Foundation, 2018, https://www.jtmestdaghfoundation.org/about/.

310. "Reading Between the Lines: How Beyond Basics Got Started," Beyond Basics, accessed August 30, 2021, https://www.beyondbasics.org/history/.

311. "Detroit Schools Score Are Lowest in the Country in Reading, Math," FOX 2 Detroit, April 11, 2018, https://www.fox2detroit.com/news/detroit-schools-score-are-lowest-in-the-country-in-reading-math.

312. "Who We Are," Beyond Basics, accessed August 30, 2021, https://www.beyond-basics.org/about/who-we-are.

313. Grace Turner and R. J. King, "Detroit's General Motors Donates $1M to Literacy Nonprofit Beyond Basics," *DBusiness*, February 3, 2020, https://www.dbusiness.com/daily-news/detroits-general-motors-donates-1m-to-literacy-nonprofit-beyond-basics/.

314. "Beyond Basics Kicks Off National Reading Month March 1 with Literacy Fundraising Gala in Detroit," *DBusiness,* February 22, 2019, https://www.dbusiness.com/daily-news/beyond-basics-kicks-off-national-reading-month-march-1-with-literacy-fundraising-gala-in-detroit/.

315. Marissa Perino and Taylor Borden, "The Late Alex Trebek Hosted More Than 8,200 'Jeopardy!' Episodes, with His Last Slated to Air on Christmas Day. Here's a Look at His Life and Legacy, from His Start as a Canadian Sports Announcer to Emmy-Winning Millionaire," *Insider,* November 24, 2020, https://www.businessinsider.com/alex-trebek-jeopardy-host-salary-age-wife-children-career-guinness-record-2019-3.

316. Theresa Tamkins, "Alex Trebek Dies After Battle with Pancreatic Cancer," *WebMD,* November 8, 2020, https://www.webmd.com/cancer/pancreatic-cancer/news/20201108/alex-trebek-dies-of-pancreatic-cancer.

317. *20/20*, season 1, episode 228, "Alex Trebek Remembered—A 20/20 Special," aired November 8, 2020, on ABC, 0:00, https://abc.com/shows/abc-news-specials/episode-guide/2020-11/08-alex-trebek-remembered-a-2020-special.

318. "Alex Trebek Remembered," 22:52.

319. "Klippel Feil Syndrome," Genetic and Rare Diseases Information Center, April 30, 2020, https://rarediseases.info.nih.gov/diseases/10280/klippel-feil-syndrome.

THE JT MESTDAGH FOUNDATION

The JT Mestdagh Foundation, established in 2018, sees a world changed and improved by children with congenital colorectal issues, who receive world-class medical care, and by those with dyslexia and other learning disabilities by supporting these children and their families facing challenges, whether it is from medical disabilities or dyslexia. JT Jester has a heart to help those in need, and his philanthropy efforts through his foundation prove this.

Explore his efforts at
www.jtmestdaghfoundation.org.